I AM YOUR BABY

MOTHER

(A Book of Poems)

Spiritual Interpretation of

Mother Child Relationship in God

Dr Antony Theodore

edited & introduced by

Dr Tapan Kumar Pradhan

Copyright © 2020 Kohinoor Books
All rights reserved.

ISBN : 978 – 81-945797-2-4

First Edition 2020

published and marketed by

KOHINOOR BOOKS
www.kohinoorbooks.com

Kohinoor Star Publications Private Limited
2293-A, REC Road, Mancheswar Rail Station
Bhubaneswar – 751 017

CONTENT

PART-III :- Mother and Child

PART-IV :- I Am Your Baby Mom
(In Translation)

ACKNOWLEDGEMENT

I owe a deep debt of gratitude to my fellow poet friends on Poemhunter website. My poetic craft has been shaped by the honest feedback received from thousands of readers. Although I have published my poems online on several websites, it is on poemhunter.com that I received wholehearted support from many kindred souls.

Protection of innocent children is the most sacred spiritual vocation of mankind. This extends to the protection of unborn embryos growing inside a woman's womb. A mother's love for her child is the greatest expression of human emotion of love on earth. This book celebrates and glorifies that highest love, which has the power to break the barrier between Man and God.

Dr Tapan Kumar Pradhan offered to present my poems in a book form. Many years ago I had requested Dr Tapan to write a few poems for me. I had also once requested him to gift a book of his choice to me. He had promised to me both. I think he has far exceeded my expectations. I have discussed with him several of my poems at length. I have also discussed with him the underlying unity among all the major religions of the world including Christianity, Hinduism and Islam. I believe that he shares my thoughts on the relevance of Christ's teachings for the modern world. I have full faith in his capacity to honestly interpret my poems.

ANTONY THEODORE

FOREWORD

This book contains sixty nine poems themed on the loving relationship between a mother and her child. These poems also symbolically represent the eternal pull of love between Man and God in the latter's aspect of Divine Mother.

A mother's love for her child is quite instinctive and natural in the animal kingdom. It is considered one of the most divine amongst all human relationships. Similar is the love of the Creator for all the created beings. Like maternal love, God's divine love cannot also be explained by human reasoning alone. Even the greatest sages have not been able to fully fathom the depths and nuances of divine love.

Just as an innocent child instinctively feels and reciprocates her mother's affection, an adult human being with a pure heart also instinctively senses the love vibrations emanating from the source of all creation. This love cannot be learnt from a book, or taught by a teacher. The love is always present, but a distracted adult mind entrenched in worldly attraction cannot immediately perceive it. When the mind gets cleared of impurities through devotion, concentration and divine grace, the full force of this love is felt intuitively in the devotee's heart.

Devotees do visualise God as Father as well as Mother. In the Holy Bible Jesus refers to God as Heavenly Father, whereas Indian sages like Ramakrishna have perceived the same God as Divine Mother. Both approaches are equally good. But in the entire animal kingdom mother-child relationship appears to be more natural and instinctive than father-child relationship. A mother never judges or punishes her prodigal child. All mistakes of the child are simply ignored by the doting mother as innocent pranks. Similarly all the sins of a devotee with contrite heart are forgiven when the latter returns to the path of God.

In this book Antony Theodore has showcased the superiority of mother-child love over all other worldy relationships. Higher evolution of humans can be possible only when people are able to extend the same kind of love to all humanity and to all created beings. Love alone can destroy all social evils and transcend all manmade limitations. This book is a humble attempt to recognise and spark the same divine love in all human hearts.

The book has four parts. Part-I deals with a child's love for its mother. The opening poem in this part is "I Am Your Baby, Mum". This is the most widely translated work in Antony's entire poetic oeuvre. Part-II deals with a mother's natural love for its child. Poems in Part-III explore the deeper spiritual truths underlying mother-child relationship. Part-IV contains translation of the eponymous very first poem in the book into many world languages. This part is included with a view to providing native speakers of different langages with a feel of Antony's seminal works in their native tongues.

Some of these poems speak againt abortion of unborn human foetuses. Many other poems voice the need for protection of children and their childhood. Anti-abortion campaign has traditionally been a Catholic Christian teaching. But this book is not on Christianity per se. Rather the book explores the universal truths in Christ's teachings which are applicable to every human civilization in all ages.

Although Jesus Christ's entire life was an embodiment of universal love, his teachings also covered various aspects of intimate human love as lay persons understand it. According to the poet, the natural attraction between a mother and her child a reflection of the universal love force immanent in all creation. Act of conceiving and giving birth to a child is not only a holy sacrament, but is also a divine form of worship. True love between an adult human couple finds fulfilment in marriage through the birth of an offspring. Extending that natural love to entire mankind is a prerequisite for attaining the highest state of God realisation.

Antony Theodore is a spiritual poet. Although he has written extensively on the scriptures of all major world religions, his meditations on Christ have been most revealing and uplifting.

Antony has written thousands of poems in different languages, although primarily he writes in English. Some of his original poems in English have been translated into other languages by native speakers and poets belonging to different countries. Many of these poems are already scattered over the internet in various forms. This book is a humble attempt to bring the best amongst all those poems under a single comprehensive organised framework. I have selected these poems on the basis of their immediate relevance to the broad theme and structure of this book. These need not be the most representative of Antony's immense poetic oeuvre.

In some of the poems included in this book, the poet has provided footnotes to throw light on the conceptualisation as well as the scriptural and historical background of the chosen topic. Occasionally I have provided additional notes to drive home the spiritual undertones of a poem. My notes essentially contain my views, and need not reflect the poet's original view on the matter.

Many of the poems have been edited by me to conform to the overall design of the book. Some poems were originally composed in free flowing passage form. These have been modified and tweaked slightly so as to have a more presentable verse form. I have been in close correspondence with the poet for almost a decade. I have discussed both poetic techniques as well as scriptural interpretation with the poet over hundreds of fruitful hours. So I have reason to believe that I understand the poet's point of view behind these verse creations. I am thankful to the poet for allowing me the liberty to freely explore and interpret these spiritual gems.

Some of the poems contained in this book have appeared in slightly different versions on various websites and online platforms. The poet has also been editing and tweaking the poems online from time to time. However, I am presenting the poems as originally received by me from the poet during my extensive correspondence.

EDITOR

ANTONY THEODORE
Life and Works

Readers worldwide have been intrigued by Dr Antony Theodore's inspiring poems on humanity, religion and spirituality. Antony's poems offer amazing clarity and insight into many cryptic messages contained in world scriptures such as Bible, Gita, Veda and Quran. The poems are very simple but original, and they contain the underlying essence of all world religions. Antony does not preach any particular doctrine. But rather the poems contain universal messages of brotherhood and love.

Who is Antony Theodore?

Dr Antony Theodore has legions of followers on various online poetry platforms. On Poemhunter website Antony is one of the topmost popular poets in the whole world. Thousands of poets and readers worldwide have read and commented on the unique and insightful spiritual gems penned by "Antony Theodore".

According to legends and hearsay Dr Antony was born as John Antony Theodore Vazhakoottathil in Alleppey district of Kerala, India. After he was orphaned in early childhood, he was nursed by his devout Catholic godmother Genova Ma. After Genova's untimely demise Antony migrated to Germany. He studied at Ludwig Maximilian University in Munich and Fordham University in New York. He reportedly obtained two bachelor's degrees in science and business administration, and later on obtained two doctoral degrees in English literature and Philosophy of World Religions.

In 1986 when he was travelling from India to Germany, Antony's flight carrying 400 passengers got hijacked at Karachi airport in Pakistan. He survived with four gunshot wounds, while 22 of his fellow passengers were killed in the 17 hour long siege. This traumatic experience turned his mind to poetry and social activism. He was ordained as a pastor and served as a chaplain in St Martin, Munich. Antony remained unmarried and spent a large part of his life in Dortmund, Germany.

However, the diligent and inquisitive readers might have already guessed that actually there is no such poet as the Christian Poet Dr Antony Theodore in the physical world in the 21st century. There is no such poet in Germany as claimed in many websites. One Fr Antony Theodore is listed in the Diocese of Alleppey, and one Pastor Antony Theodore Vazhakoothathil in listed in the pastoral team of Dortmund. The list of persons injured in the 1986 Pan Am flight hijack at Karachi (en route to Frankfurt from Mumbai) also contains a person named Father Anthony Theodore. However none of these persons correspond to the poet writing under the pseudonym of Dr Antony Theodore aka Tony Brahmin on Poem Hunter and myriad other poetry websites. When I first came across Antony's poems on internet, I did extensive search online to identify the person. A careful scrutiny of the poems clearly points to the poet's Indian roots and family connections with the Kashmir province of India.

Hemangi Sharma as Tony Brahmin

Dr Antony Theodore is none other than the Indian mystic poet Hemangi Sharma. This is a truth which was known only to me till date. This is because Hemangi Sharma never liked to publish poems under her own name. She had various reasons for doing so. Hemangi has written thousands of poems under hundreds of different pseudonyms such as Lalitha Iyer and Poet Poet etc. Antony Theodore is her pseudonym or fake ID under which she has published her interpretation of Jesus Christ's universal teachings on Poemhunter and other online poetry platforms. In routine online correspondence with fellow poets Antony Theodore invariably uses the nickname Tony Brahmin, which reflects Hemangi Sharma's Indian origin as someone born in a traditional Kashmir Brahmin family.

The Epilogue to this book contains details of Hemangi Sharma's extensive poetic works under various pseudonyms on poemhunter and other websites. Further details on Hemangi Sharma's extraordinary relationship with me can be found in my book *I, She and the Sea*.

What is Antony's Religion?

Antony Theodore primary writes on Christian values. In her poems the birth, wanderings, teaching, suffering, crucifixion and resurrection of Jesus Christ have been tellingly re-enlivened. However "Antony" does not profess any particular religion. Her poems bring forth the universal truths common to all world religions. Therefore Antony is as much a Hindu and Muslim as she is a Christian, Buddhist and Confucian. Her poems are a constant reminder to humanity to rise above narrow boundaries of caste, creed, race and religion, and to work towards universal brotherhood and world peace.

INTRODUCTION

Antony Theodore's poems are deceptively simple. The diction is easy and natural, and the words are from everyday common parlance. But these plain simple words have the power to profoundly affect the human heart in subtle ways. A telling example is the eponymous poem in this book titled "I Am Your Baby, Mum". Thousands of readers have reported how the poem has changed their perception towards the unborn foetus. Sometimes the impact is felt months or years after reading a poem.

Symbolism of Christ

Many of the poems in this book have made allusions to the Baby Jesus born to Virgin Mary. Virgin birth of "Christ" symbolises that human soul has directly descended from God. Jesus in his physical human form graced this earth for a brief period of thirty three years at the beginning of the modern Christian era. The four books of the New Testament of Holy Bible throw light on only the birth, infancy and the last few years of his ministry. The Gospel is silent on the intervening years of Jesus's extraordinary life. However the surviving records of his teachings as gleaned from those few years of his life have had a profound effect on the shaping of world history. The momentous impact of that one human life is still being felt in the unfolding of human civilisation. That extraordinary impact emanates from the unparalleled purity, truth and love manifested in the unblemished life of Jesus the Christ.

Jesus apparently spoke to his disciples in the ancient Aramaic language. The teachings have been carried forth by the apostles and missionaries to the furthest corners of the world in several different languages. The teachings have been translated and re-translated hundreds of times, finally culminating in the authorised King James version, which is the most widely accepted version today. However, much of the original teachings have been distorted and lost through the translations.

Antony Theodore's poems do not preach any particular faith or religion. They delve much deeper than the surface meaning of Biblical texts. The poems dwell on the universal message of love and brotherhood contained in the Gospel, which is the same as that expressed through the Vedas, Gita, Quran and other world scriptures.

For instance, we may take the expression "Word of God" as mentioned in the Bible. Its exact equivalent in Vedic Sanskrit is "Shabda Brahman" – i.e. Word-God. However, Shabda in Sankrit has two different meanings – Word as well as Sound. In the original Aramaic version of Jesus's sayings, Word of God would have symbolised the primordial sound of creation (Aum-Amen-Amin) which permeates the entire universe. However, translated into modern English, Word merely connotes the written word as a combination of the letters of alphabet. This may compel a religious fanatic to go by the exact written texts without bothering to understand their inner spiritual connotations. This can have both funny as well as ridiculously disastrous consequences. For example, "breaking bread" can mean taking dinner, cutting a loaf or even holy communion. It may be noted that at the Last Supper Jesus had given bread to his disciples saying "this is my body" and then gave them wine saying "this is my blood". Hence when we find use of words like bread, wine, fish and sheep in the Bible, we must understand that they have meanings other than their dictionary meanings. And the same applies to the scriptures of other religions also. Much of the scriptural writings are in the form of proverbs and allusions. By piercing through the external verbal gloss if we can arrive at the originally intended meanings, we shall find that scriptures of all world religions essentially speak the same One Truth.

Similar is the case with other Biblical expressions like Garden, Star, Flesh, Shepherd etc and Quranic expressions like Moon, Horse, Night and Dawn etc. In the original Aramaic the meanings of these words would have been quite different from what they ordinarily connote today. The present book does not attempt to dig out the original meanings through phonetic or lexical re-interpretation. It merely acknowledges that the inner meanings of scriptures can be quite different from the surface meaning of the text.

Scope of the Book

The poems in this volume have been arranged under four different parts of almost equal lengths. Part-I starts with the poem "I Am Your Baby, Mum", which has been translated into more than twenty different world languages. This part also includes a few poems on Jesus' miraculous conception and birth through the virgin mother Mary. On a metaphysical level this symbolises "birth" of the desire for emancipation taking root in the adult human heart.

The second part of the book titled "Love You, My Child" dwells on the mother's expresion of love for her child. Poems like "My Unborn Baby" and "Thirsting for a Baby" depict the barren emptiness of conjugal human love unless it culminates in a baby. It symbolises the utter futility of all worldy pursuits which do not trigger spiritual aspirations in the human heart.

The third part titled "Mother and Child" explores the deeper spiritual truths underlying this divine relationship. The poem "Mother of a School Going Son" is a telling testament of the supreme sacrifice made by a mother for her child without any expectation of reciprocation or return.

The fourth part contains translations of the eponymous first poem in the book – perhaps Antony's most celebrated poem – into several world languages. I have translated the poem into French, Hindi and my own mother tongue Odia. Other poets from different countries have translated it into their respective languages.

The Epilogue presents revealing facts regarding the true identity of Antony Theodore. Most readers would find it quite shocking, to say the least. I thought it was my duty to disclose the identity of this truly world class poet, so that people worldwide can appreciate the extraordinary range of the poet's compositions.

The Appendix includes two other poignant poems by Antony for supplementary reading. The poem "Mom's Last Smile" has been translated by the poet herself into German – albeit under yet another pseudonym of Me Poet Yeps Poet. Perhaps she did so to further complicate her narrative that she was a German native. But Hemangi Sharma is well versed in many languages. Her free translation shows her versatility in composing the same poem differently in different languages.

The last poem in the book titled "If You Die Before Me" has multiple layers of meanings. The poem dwells on a traditional folk belief that a woman has to suffer in hell if she dies before her earthly lover does. But when juxtaposed against the context of this book, the poem takes on entirely new meanings. For instance, if a woman kills her unborn baby, it is the baby who should reach heaven first while the guilt-ridden mother experiences hell on earth.

Message for Humanity

All the poems in the book celebrate and glorify the tender human emotion of love. The most divine expression of this love is seen in the mother-child relationship, since it is a near perfect reflection of the eternal relationship between Man and his Creator. By loving another human being, one expresses love for the Supreme Lover who is present in all hearts. Marriage of a man and woman is also an expression of that divine love which finds fulfilment in the birth of a love child. Conceiving a baby, giving birth and protecting a child through adulthood are all symbolic of the devotee harbouring divine aspirations in his heart and then nurturing that ardent aspiration through ceaseless spiritual practices till the attainment of final enlightenment. The "baby" in this book is symbolic of the nascent spiritual aspirations in the human heart. Abortion of an embryo is symbolic of aborting one's spiritual quest before attaining God realisation.

The suffering multitude of humanity is waiting for the Second Coming of Christ for spiritual redemption. It is believed that the second coming will not be a physical resurrection of the human body of a historical Jesus, but rather a spiritual awakening within each human being. This is the very essence of Antony Theodore's poetry. These poems call out to the readers to shed their limiting individual ego and to merge themselves in the eternal bliss of ever expanding God communion.

PART - I

I LOVE YOU, MOTHER

NAKED IN LAP OF NATURE

AND A BABY IS BORN

Truth is naked. Truth was, is and will ever be. But we humans like to wear masks.

To perceive pure love that is God, you have to unmask your heart, unmask your soul, unmask the purity of your being.

Mind, reasoning and all sensory knowledge are only stumbling blocks in realising the pure purity of being. When you realise this simple truth, you give up all thinking. And when you give up thinking the ugly clothing will fall down. The naked cabaret dancer will start dancing. Beauty will flow, hearts will smile, penetrating your being with knives and organs made of pure energy. Then a little baby you will become. Like amoeba, you are the mother, you are the kid. A baby heart you need to receive the full force of God's Love.

For when God's light opens my heart, I hear the laughter of innocence in my being.

> when rain drops
> touched my dry cups
> made of mud
> I became mad
> so sweet was the first touch
> wow, I can hear you
> whisper much, much…

I AM YOUR BABY, MUM

I am your baby Mum
I did not come on my own Mum
God's angels flew down to your womb
From the mighty heavens
And placed me in your holy womb

I did not come on my own mum;
God wanted it so.

I was so happy in my new cave of love
In your holy womb
And slept there peacefully
The angles watched
They prayed
To keep me safe always
Till I will be born on the face of the earth

They practiced heavenly songs of birth
to play on their golden harps on my birthday

When I was sleeping in your womb
The angels used to come to me
You did not know it, my dearest Mum

I was happy to be born
as your beloved child

I wanted to smile
I wanted to sing
I wanted to play
I wanted to suck your breast milk

Until you were satisfied
I wanted to see the smile on your face
When I suck all your milk from your loving breasts

They were my dreams in your womb, Mum

But on a cruel day
you decided to kill me

The devils in the Hades
heard about your decision
They brought the loudest drums
played in the devilish rhythms
All the devils came together,
came and danced in circles,
jumping and singing
They danced in lines
They danced in circles
They danced on the toes
They danced on their heads
They sang the wildest of songs
and the devil drummers played
The whole hell was happy
that you decided to kill me

You know how much I cried?
You know how many angels cried?
Do you know how the whole heaven cried
on my day of death in your holy womb?

A moment before i was cruelly murdered
I saw the All-Powerful God crying helplessly.

TEACH NOT BIRDS TO SWIM

Teach not a flying bird to swim
Ask not a bird to burrow
It will break its beaks and wings.

Force not the eagle to swim
Like a fish - its world is the sky.

Teach not a bird to climb
A monkey can do much better.

Train not the rabbit to fly
Ask not the squirrel to bark.

Let the peacock dance
Ask not the hen to waltz

Train not the monkey to sing
Nightingale will croon for you.

O Teachers, O Mothers
If only you knew
Creative potential of us little humans
God entrusted to you !!!

(Poet's Note :- Our schools and universities fail to understand the special creative capabilities of our students. We have to create a positive atmosphere and believe that each and every student entrusted to us is a unique being. Our children have greatness in them and very special talents. Parents should begin it in the family and teachers and professors should continue to challenge and provoke them to get the best out of their uniqueness. It is our sublime duty to the younger generation).

MOTHER NIGHTINGALE

O Nightingale, dear Nightingale
Will you be my nightingale
For a night?
At the end of this night
I want to be reborn
As a little nightingale
In your garden of light

Sing to me, mother
Songs of your soul
I know you are there
I know you are here
Bring me peace
Bring me joy
Sing me to sleep
With your sweetest song

Sing to me
From my heart's core
In your garden of light
Let me soar.

REVEAL YOURSELF, MOTHER

From my mother's breasts
flows love and peace
like a river in full flow
like a stream in torrents
under the sun's glow

On her breasts alone
shall I sleep cuddled
like the nursing infant
in her lap fondled
by her hands to sleep
tears shall I weep

Reveal to me O Mother
Reveal yourself to me
Reveal your true love
Reveal your bounties

when I kneel in prayer
before your altar
reveal yourself
to me.

MOTHER, MAKE ME YOUR CLAY

Allow me to be the clay
in your soft loving hands
mother let me forever play
in your warm verdant lap
not on dreary desert sands

Play on my mind and heart
as you play my body Mother
like a masterful player
beat me down as you like
knead me, guide me
to shape me as you wish

I shall become that
what you want me to be

Only then I shall find
real and eternal joy
in the cooling comfort
of your loving shelter

Mother beat me down
crush me, possess me
shape me, reshape me
and make me your own.

SUN KISSED ON WAY TO SCHOOL

The tropical sun kisses me
on both my cheeks today
as I go talking and chatting
to the flitting butterflies
on the way to my school

I feel the warmth in my hairs
like dark skinned forest leaves
I hear the music of the leaves
when wind blows on them

I imagine they are being caressed
by your soft loving hands, mother
the trees, the leaves and the wind
and I want to be the summer wind

flying along the swaying leaves
and making them dance
to the undulating tunes
of my whistling breeze
and making them smile

softly with me.

YOU ARE MY HIDING PLACE

You are my hiding place
You are my secret cave

There I light my oil lamp
with oil of my heart
night after night
after sleepless nights

I sit in meditation, mother
I cogitate on your wonders
and on my beads i recite
your name a million times
about your love that flows
like oil into my lowly heart

I prostrate here, mother
in my lone secret cave
adoring you the whole night

You are my hiding place
where i seek my soul love
night after night
after sleepless nights.

MOUTHS OF CHRIST

Mama you told us
in our childhood :
Remember, my child
all mouths are your
brothers and sisters

You cannot put something
in your own greedy mouth
without giving something
to someone somewhere
who is hungry and thirsty

each child that has not smiled
each child that goes without food
is also a child of your mother
whom you have neglected

Even through hardship of poverty
and the lowly depths of adversity
Mama, you formed in us habits
and loving actions of charity
for all our brothers and sisters
born with the love of Christ.

I AM YOUR SON AND DAUGHTER

I am your child, mother
I know not my gender
I know not my religion
I know not my father

Like a son comforted
by his mother's smile
shall I comfort you
in your ripe old age
like a pure daughter
of your loving heart
I shall caress you
till eternity in love

Give me the strength, mother
to love you with all my strength.

O MY LOST MOTHER

Dear mother, when you died
did you sit upon the bud
or did you took the form of a bird
or did you swim deep into the sea
or up in the clouds into a bright new star

yesterday when I looked above
you smiled with your silvery eyes
all day when I gaze around
you seemed to whisper from the trees
the leaves sing and the scars heal
where did you go to form the new role?
oh my dear mother, canst you tell me a fool.

All night I looked among the stars
to see you special like the cartoon hours
I peer into every kitten and pup around
their eyes never show or did all show
your soft kindness and loving heart
oh my dear mother where did you go?
In this world of lonely thoughts
leaving me just innocent and simpleton fool.

WHEN YOU WALKED ME TO SCHOOL

Passion fruits, mummy
purple and shiny,
velvety blue wild olives,
inky little violet flowers
wild berries and blackberries
stimulated my taste buds
oh! I remember, mummy
those were the sweet days
when we went to school.

The years have gone by
big buildings peep up
in to the smoking sky,
mended, cobbled lane
has disappeared.

Motor cars, yellow buses
and their proud owners
fly past on the road
where we walked
in our lost childhood
hand in hand, mummy.

I wonder what the kids do now
on their way to school

I AM A CHILD OF GOD

Suffer the contempt
of your so called modern
and sophisticated world

Be true to your own self
and to dear Lord God
who created you

Do not abort me, mother
I am a child of God
I came to you seeking love
I desire nothing
God has left plenty for me
but I am seeking only
your warmth, your love

Let the world consider you a fool
but your conscience will smile
and angels of heaven will all smile
with you and with your love's child
whom you saved from destruction.

O MOTHER, MUMMY, AMMA

When the world was sleeping
you were with pain writhing;

When the world was dancing
you were carrying your weight menacing

from the prison dark
as the life form embarked
from the unseen micro cells
when one by one visible limbs shaped
into a figure of dentity and entity
your days in prison you counted
weighed down by the precious bomb
miracles breathed life into the womb
mystery and history sprinkled hope
and expression and scope
from a battle of blood and pain
born is the being of Creator's vein

Mother, mummy, mum, mama, Amma
the way the cat adores its new born
the dog, the tiger and the lion
the hapless deer mother
the birds' mothers and
beautiful Kangaroo Mum
how many mothers are in the world
how many are their species, their numbers
their modes of caring, milking, fondling
now as I watch you go into labour
as my possessive expectant mother
warding off the world around you

your instinct's offensive spikes gain ground
you instantly repulse with vehement resolve
all evil eyes looming with threats all around

Poor motherhood
the raging war within
restless urge to spare
her genre of scare
from nothing into something that dares

the heartless killers' urge to finish
and the mother's desperacy to preserve
death and birth coined by same God
bad and good bedded side by side
the hand that saves, and hand that shaves
mother - she smells her little infant born
licks with love scented with mission inborn
Mother, you who lit the lamp of my eyes
milked me with love in my tender days
and spaced a whole world in your heart
for every kid with special sweetness and art

O Mother, at the feet of Motherhood
Lies the feet of Divinity incarnate
You are the giver of my childhood
Supreme reality of innocent tranquility
Seeded with emotions of eternal perpetuity.

MY KANGAROO MUM

Wow! wow
my poor mum
she carries in and out
inside the unborn
outside the new born
the poor mum
she hops with loads
the weighing belly
dampens not
her urge to find
greener grounds

still i wonder
my heart with pity
moved, totally moved am I
the mammal's plight
the saddening sight
new milk for new born
old milk for the sister born
how could the poor being
manage the burden of offsprings

sweet little hopping bag
jumping around in tender laps
baby wonders
mum surrenders
baby's pride
mum's stride
baby's magic globe
mum's battling throb.......

HOLD MY HANDS, MOM

Oh mom,
hold my hands
while you guide my life
with the lantern's light
darkness you wipe
and show me with love
the path ahead
teach me each new thorn
which will bleed
my tender acorn
tell me mother
which is my father?
who is there among the males
who will not bed me at any style?
who can I trust
who will never fail me
and forsake when I defeated flee
Hold my hands, Mom
in your graceful steps
while I learn the world's ways
your looks and laughs hide
the darkness harbouring
every turn in life
I am but a baby of ignorance
carry me to your land of safety
let me sleep in peace and purity.

BREASTS THAT FED ME

I was born
to you my mother at night
poor thing you woke all night
sleepless you suffered
in agony and plight

I sucked you too much
you grew pail and powerless
your calcium I suckled
your firm joints grew supple

I grew upon your energy
Parasite was I
licking your life and verdour
you slowly waned and waxed off
your beautiful youth gave away
as I bloomed up

Before I die I offer my prayers
before the hand that made me stand
the breasts that fed my hunger
the tender globe that my aboard lingered

Before I die I shall kneel down
to wipe off the blood you shed
as I came out of your womb in dread
I offer my life to you, mother
you who were to me the world
for the world is nothing now I learn
but only zoomed image of a mother's pain.

As I travel over the entire world
and meet the wealthy and the mighty
at last I begin to discover the truth
that mother is the start and end
of all my life's frenzied search
she who gave me eyes and ears
and life and music of life bears
the whole secret of life lived
in her compassionate tears.

MUM MAKES ME SMILE

Mum, you make me smile.
When you kiss the sole of my foot
You make me smile.
When you kiss my little stomach
and look deep into my eyes
with such a great love
you make me smile.

When you tickle me always
and love to see me laughing
lost in your loving hands
you make me smile.

When I bite on your nipples
you are angry with me.
But even in that anger
there is tender love.
You make me smile Mummy.

You are my God
I shall know God
only through this love
that you give me day and night.

Your smile and playfulness,
your tender care,
gladness pure
will always remain in me
as the character of God.

You are a great Theologian
and a wise philosopher.
With your smiling 'hi, hu, hum',
humming and giggling with me
You teach me the Philosophy of Love.

Mummy my dearest
how can I see you again?

In the depths of the night
I open my window
and pray to the stars
Please send me my mother
Only once if possible
Only once...., I pray in earnest

O heavenly stars
ask God to send me
my mother dearest

I want to smile with her again
I want to smile with her again".

Poet's Note :- My dearest Mummy died of cancer at the age of 38. Her name is
Genova and i call her Maaaaaaa)

Editor's Note :- The poet never had a physical mother named Genova. Both
parents of the poet were still alive on the date of publication of this book. This poem
had been written at least five years earlier.

MY BABY DREAMS

When I sleep
you send me dreams
dressed in love
you appear now
and sit upon
my silver tresses
and slyly caress
my silky bosom
and look into
my heart
with a magnifying lens
enlarging everything
as I close
my eye-keys
you steal and
shut out my looks
to outside world;

in my slumber
you treat me a baby
and make me wish
that I am your loveliest dish
like a stream
you glide into me
and I helpless
enjoy the show
that I do miss
the nights you are amiss
yet, how the stage is set
and you crown me inset..
I wonder,

how you appear in my dreams
and fake me with fancies
you desire,
and smell my heart
inching every second
a little bit
day by day
melting my obstinacies
and painting my inner urges
into a larger canvas
and magnifying my
unseen passions
highlighting the
shy delicacies.

I BECAME A BABY AGAIN

I lost my old mother
and her little love world;
but the dreams she did cherish
I won't allow them to perish

she showed me the sun
and its perpendicular rays
golden lines drawn in our kitchen forays
the dust of life dancing on it in arrays

she made me love the stars and moon
jasmine and night air stirring me soon
I too sang with her those romantic notes
lyrics of past full of love and harmony boasts.

mother made me realise
how sweet is the world of wise
no killing and bleeding,
but loving and hugging
Wise love and kiss hearts, unbugging others.

She showed me how wealthy are the wealthy
who love and are kind and make things around healthy
who live with every baby and bathe with every rain
in every blade of green, she showed me fertile brain

Now as I loose my memory and sanity
my ability to understand mundanity
in a commercial world full of warring insanity
I become a baby again, dear mother
full of frights and fears in a nightie.

I AM STILL A BABY

Jump, oh no
slowly skating down ages
life refolds
passions untold
pressing out
like the cycle tube
aired with;

slowly I feel
how I was washed and cleansed
how I learnt to learn
what life and lust is all about
how I understood
how intentions good and bad
make one feel sick
and love of human hearts
how the same act
with good intent
make it holy and unholy and cheap
when acted with intentions third rate

when like the carpet unfurled
I skated down my memory lane
I saw poor me with wonders agog
not knowing what to do with the flooding teens
how to handle with emotions uncontrolled
and even do not know how to make out
what I myself, my growing physique meant to me
equations unsolved, I banged my head and heart
to walls of thoughts and hurt and wounded and scarred
now I could watch like a photo shot

series of myself down the lane
answers in my purse now
whereas the poor me in different stages
had blundered and blanked and backed out in ages
foolish, idiotic and insensibly hurt by crowds and fantasies.

time has flown, yet I have grown little
still I speak to the crows and talk with the squirrels
crazy after running mongoose and chirping birdies
still I wonder who sits upon those cloudy pillows
and why full moon is always beautiful
and what makes the greens sing and ponds swollen
why rain loves to make muds fragrant
and birds wet without any protest
still a baby I watch nature with amazing eyes
still I don't understand the invisible nature
that makes me happy and giggle like a mad.

MOTHER CAME IN A CHARIOT

It was a glorious sunset
with waves playing on my feet
gold, red, yellow and amber
as I watched those rays
sucked me in delicate passion.

Their chariot of flames
flew down to me
flames around, all around
golden blue and red
with gleaming eyes I saw

Seven white winged horses
flew into my presence at the shore.

I saw mummy in the chariot,
smiling like the morning sun.

My eyes opened as sunflowers do
with moonlit eyes
pouring out pure blooms of bliss
she whispered to me softly

In joy immeasurable
her voice melted
in hugs and kisses
she murmured in my little ears
'You are my treasure, the apple of my eye'.

She adorned me with the stars,
blessed me with tenderness,

filled me with treasures divine.

I was blissful,
serene and desireless

Singing a glorious hymn
pouring on me her sweetest perfume,
she touched my life from the chariot.

The chariot flew away.

Every dusk,
and every night,
I look at the stars
and murmur:
O twinkling stars!
send my mummy again to me.

I sleep.
Tear drops linger on my lashes.

(Poet's Note :- It is a pleasant vision of my dearest Ma (in Hindi language we call
mother so lovingly Maaaaaa). I lost her when i was in the school. She had cancer
and died at the age of 38. I yearn for her presence even now every day. It is a
great loss i suffered and i will not be cured from the wounds that is created by her
absence. When I see the sunset my heart raises itself to her chariot).

Editor's Note :- Hemangi Sharma was not bereaved of her mother at the time of
writing this poem. She composed it in September 2010. Here the poet Antony
clearly admits that her mother tongue was Hindi. Hence he was an Indian and not
German.

MY MOTHER – WOMAN OF THE DAY

You taught me love
simple, innocent, pure
you taught me to be kind
to birds, squirrels and street dogs
you taught me how to draw
simple kinter garden things
little everything amazing
you taught me sing
to enjoy your own voice sweet
you taught me songs
to feel divinity at the tip of your throbs
you taught me to voice my voice
and feel expression of infinite
float through the air around humming and bright
you taught me to draw, I said
but I forgot to finish it
thus you took me ahead
from creator's start to end
first from simple sketches
and last to full flowing peacocks
first from Darwin's single celled
to find drawing, painting and sketches
in clouds, sky, earth and land
water and empty airs too at last
you taught me to draw with pencil and paper
then I learnt that drawings do not need either
you can draw with your heart
in others heart, the art of love

which alone is eternal
of all beautiful drawings in the world

be it Da Vinci or Van Gogh
or my dear Ravi Varma's
the most carved out etching
the most beautiful drawing
is the one carved in a heart
by another kind heart
with paint of love and pencil of feeling

So my mother, dear mother
you are my woman of this day
and for ages to come
and till eternity
i am in love with you

MY MOTHER AND FOR THAT SAKE ALL MOTHERS,
MOTHERS OF ALL BEINGS, ARE MY WOMEN OF THE DAY.

Editor's Note :- This poem was written by Hemangi Sharma on March 7, 2016. I had sent her a series of poems on Womanhood on that day.)

Kinter Garden :- Kindergarten deliberately twisted – typical of Hemangi Sharma's poetic style.

PART – II

LOVE YOU, MY CHILD

A MOTHER'S GIFT OF ETERNITY

HUNGRY WITH LOVE

For ages I have been kept hungry and imprisoned in a cave. Now you are filling the parched deserted heart with heavenly ambrosia. Oh god, when divine energies flood in, what could mortal souls say. Now you are feeding this famished soul, whose intestine's capacity is just a hole of blue sky and a pinch of golden sun light. You are filling my whole with ocean of love when my heart's capacity is that of a newborn baby to suckle just a drop of its flavour.

I am every day morning brushing their teeth, oiling their hair, combing, powdering, milking them, feeding them, clothing them, caressing and fondling them, laugh with them, show them sky, birds, mongoose, owls, bats and all that my eyes could see, sing songs to them, kiss them with my loving heart. What not I do for them. Now when I open my heart and show to you, you say oh, it is only a shoe flower..."

     so sweet my dear
     when I skate upon
     your tender wonder la
     tempting me beyond
     I forget myself and
     my life and all
     when I sweetly feel
     thine tender throbs
     the heart of life
     blossoms wild
     when I land upon
     the heaps of love
     soft and silky, satiny milky

I AM YOUR LOVING MOTHER

I am your mother, loving and holy
Come and suckle from my breasts
Until you are no more thirsty
From these consoling breasts
You can savour always in delight

Mine are glorious breasts
You are my beloved one
My child born in intimate love
To whom shall I offer my breasts
If not for you always and ever more

Like a son comforted by his mother
Shall I comfort you
Like a daughter of her heart
I shall caress you in love.

At my sight your heart will rejoice
Your sinews will attain strength
Your lips will sing of eternal love
Your bones will flourish like the grass.

I AM YOUR HIDING ANGEL

I am your angel, my baby
May I stay in your heart
as an angel under cover
No one knows I am here

When you cry I will feel your pain
When it is dark in your heart
I shall bring little twinkling stars

When tears flow down your cheeks
I will come unseen to wipe your tears

I shall invite the nightingales
to sing and make you happy
I shall sing in your ears
my sweetest lullaby
when nightingales sleep
I shall sing

And when you are asleep
I shall kiss your sweet lips
until you dream of flowers
birds, skies, heavenly beings.

(Poet's Note :- This was published in Poetfreak under the name of Genova Maa.
Genova was my beloved mother. She died at the young age of 38. I want to keep
her name alive as long as I am alive).

Editor's Note :- Antony Theodore (Hemangi Sharma) did not have a physical
mother named Genova. Both the parents of the poet were alive, both sixty plus, at
the time of publication of this poem. The poet may be referring to Genova in a
symbolic manner.

RING NOW THE BELLS

The dawn bird sings
morning light pours in
wake up my little one
time of lullaby is gone

Take your rose dear
in your little hand
Give me your smile
walk in the path all bright
leading to never ending light

Seek a place your own
where you can store up
the secrets of your soul
of joy, sorrow and valor

Come and ring the bells
that sound into the depths
of your righteous soul
where you can hear the call
of the one whom your heart loves

The one whom your heart loves.

COME, TOUCH ME

Touch me
here, like this

Touch me
to feel the life
within you.

Touch me
Once more
Again and again
Come touch me, baby
Like this

Only when you go out
of your own self

to touch, to feel

only then
will you
know
what is love.

AND THE MOON SMILED

In tiptoeing tiny steps
I came to you
to pluck your soul
in the middle of night

You found me, hugged me
and then kissed me
you squeezed my cheeks

like this

And then you rose
from your soft dream bed
you plucked your soul
and gave it to me
and then the moon smiled.

Poet's Note :- True love experience is always a mystery. "The smile of the moon"
- the mild golden light of the moon that falls in the garden on the riverbanks was
always mysterious for me.)

COME WITH ME, BABY

Come we shall swim
This ocean of love
Have no fear now
I am with you always
Like your loving mother

Come, we shall swim away
and alight together
on the other shore
when we reach that shore
I shall help you climb
on rainbows with me

We shall be in light
clad in colors of joy
in smiles, in peace
we shall then embrace
and kiss cheek to cheek
as the angels of heaven
will all be watching us
in silent wonderment

Come we shall swim
This ocean of love.

MY RED UMBRELLA

With my red umbrella
I stood alone in the rain
in my secret garden
crying behind my umbrella
imploring for mercy
for all the sins I committed

This Christmas day
when Jesus is born
the innocent baby
in gutter poverty
I cry behind
my red umbrella.

Oh I love your birth
I kneel before you
O Lord of the universe,
forgive me my sins
of aborting my own children

Many a time i did
this horrible sin
I hear them crying
in my sacred womb

Baby my beloved one
in Bethlehem,
forgive me
forgive me
forgive me.

i am hiding now, baby
under my red umbrella,
symbol of the blood
of the babies i poured
inside my womb.

forgive me Baby
forgive me.

DO NOT CRY MY BABY

Don't cry baby
let tears not come into your eyes
wipe them away
don't cry just for me today

I want to see love in your eyes
rose's blue bells and daffodils
with the fragrance of my love

O why do you cry
here still am I
O babe don't cry
wipe out the tear
from your eye

I am still alive

why fear of what docs say
they have to calm you one day
so here as I sing for you
dear babe just stand by

hold my hand and press it hard
so I'll know you love me so

O babe don't cry
for me just smile
as I stay longer
just long enough
to stay with you for a while
just to see your glamorous smile

O baby don't cry
in peace let me die
let not tears
Come into your eye

I am here for you today
my babe!
do not cry.

I SHALL NEVER LEAVE YOU

Come baby
come my sweet one
i shall hug you
in my waiting arms
i shall sing you to sleep
in my comforting hands
you are mine
oh dear all mine
I shall never leave you.

Sleep, sleep, sleep
in my loving hands
you are so dear to me
You are mine, all mine
I shall never leave you.

I AM THE WOMB

I am the goal of life,
the Lord Mother
and support of all,
I am the inner witness,
the abode of all.

I am the source of life
the Divine Mother
and lover of all
I am the inner secret
the light for all.

I am the only refuge,
the one true friend;
I am the beginning,
I am the staying,
and the end of creation;

I am the womb
and the eternal seed.

MY WOMB IS SACRED

We sense
a swelling
of the Spirit
a growing awareness
of the inner call
to come forward
and take a stand
for those who cannot
stand for themselves
to be a voice for them
for the small and silent
a light for those ones
in the sacred darkness
of the womb.

Come my little one
fear not the world
my womb is sacred
find your inner call
fight out of darkness
baby of my womb
live in your glory
and make my life
as a mother sacred.

I FORMED YOU IN THE WOMB

I knew you
I formed you
in my dark womb
from a little seed
to a smiling plant
of brightness
I carved you
of sweet love

I bore you, baby
I raised you
to my ample breasts
from a little sapling
to a leafy tall tree
I watched you grow
on my milk of love

You are my beloved
I have lots of plan for you
You are mine
You shall live
You shall grow
to your fullness
your full divinity
to proclaim
the goodness
of the Lord
God in all.

SHE IS MINE

She is mine
She is my beloved
She is my little angel
Don't mess up with her skirt
She is mine
I will protect her
even if I will have to be killed.

She is my joy
She is beauty divine
She is my little queen
Don't meddle with her heart
She is mine
I will cherish her
ever till I live, till I die.

MINE ARE GLORIOUS BREASTS

Come, savour my glorious breasts
these living fountains of limitless bliss
filled with nectar brewed in heaven
into the bread, fish and wine of life

Come suck to your heart's fill
do not hesitate, drink it all
my child born in intimate love
to you alone I offer my milk

Feel the elixir of life
flow into your heart
from the endless chalice
of my glorious breasts

At their very sight your heart will rejoice
your legs will gain speed, arms strength
your flesh will glow like the morning sun
your bones will flourish like the high seas.

Editor's Note :- This poem is a variation of the earlier one titled "I Am Your Loving Mother".

MY UNBORN BABY

Every secret is written in those palms
only if the baby unfolds it can I see
but the baby is not born.

Every code is written in those hands
only if the baby wakes up then i can see
but the baby is sleeping.

All future in black and white
beautifully lined in those whites
but the baby refuses to open.

It is not ripe yet
it is not time yet
baby bubbles sweetly
and smiles discreetly.

Every dawn I wonder if that leaf will unfold
the big big leaf of plaintain tree yonder
it is a beauty to see the curled rod of leaf unopened
unstretched it is a lovely sight; yet if only it spreads its chest
oh, I could see the vision that appears in my dreams in mist.

Edtor's Note :- Hemangi Sharma wrote it on June 20, 2015 – about a month before
she met me physically for the first time. By this time she had already discussed her
plans of raising a baby girl with me.

I LOVE MY NAUGHTY BOY

I have a naughty boy
and a naughty boy he is
he loves playing pranks
and a Comedian sorts he is.

I am now a mother old
weak and fatigued too
but I love my boy's tricks
and his prickly intelligence
with lovely poetic inks.

I love him very very much
though I do not show it out
I love his comedies and jokes
and all his harmless pranks
upon my greying old brains.

I love him so purely that
my air and water and fire smells of him
my thoughts and dreams
and walks and songs he is
I am but composed of him
bulging bulky am I.

Editor's Note :- Hemangi Sharma wrote this poem on March 7, 2016 which was International Woman's Day. I had sent her a series of poems on Woman on that day. Her poems were in response to my poems.)

Air, Water, Fire :- Three of the five primordial elements of universe as per Hindu philosophy (other two being earth, sky). This shows Antony's Indian heritage.

Lovely ink :- Allusion to my poems which she loved

WHERE IS MY BABY

Barren am I
my babies dont come out
just they dont sprout
my ovums
they dont fuse
I am confused;
I loved him
we kissed in the corridors
and in the beaches
all night long
we did not miss
we made love
with wonderful moves
learnt from the books
teaching sex tricks
yet, my baby
it is not coming out.
We met in the teens
when roses bulbed
in my inner beans
he learnt to draw
my naked in raw
my body a straw
and lust flirted without flaw

yet, my baby
it did not come out
we made it
again and again
but my baby
it did not come out.....

THIRSTING FOR A BABY

Dry am I
deceived of life
my thirsty hours
need some showers

the heart is wanting
pure hours of joy
but brain is famished
of ideas to toy

body is sick
of silent tortures
pricking here and
paining there

the labour I do
nobody grades
my efforts of strain
all in vain

I love to breed
but only lust
I share
to reap only dust

God is silent
watching vigilant
my stumbles
he studies in tables

why do I live

when my mind is thirsty
my joints are unhealthy
and reason unworthy

give me some life
let me thrive
fetch me a babe's body
let me undress
and clothe in rhapsody.

MY WOMB IS WET WITH MY KID

I am really wet
the rain came in summer
when the heat was on
and my body ailed
with the inner dryness
I started ageing
for want of love
my hair greying
roots fraught with thoughts
and when I started sinking
with every dawn
difficult to wake up
my body from the frozen bed
when my limbs wont obey
orders of my brains
then, the rains came
out of nowhere
like an angelic beauty
the message of love
from the blues of skies
bulging clouds
blessing with drops
each drop
inhaled
perfuming me
with the scent of earth.

Earth is wet
I too
she is ready to sprout
but I have to wait

her seeds come out fast
mine takes time to surface
my love implanted
I am pregnant
Yeah, I am pregnant
I want to shout
in everyone's ears
lest they fail to hear
I am carrying
the baby of a Summer Rain
and I am not tired
I am full of richness
Creativity inside me
It is kidding me
yes, I am a Kid now
babying a Kid
in my wetted womb.

SLEEP BABY

Sleep baby sleep
May I sing a lullaby

I am your mum now
I am your dad now
I am your angel of love

I shall protect you always
You are safe in my hands.

I shall hug you softly
You can sleep on my chest
Like a cat curled

Sleep baby sleep

PART – III

MOTHER AND CHILD

TWO HALVES OF ONE GOD

TWO HALVES OF ONE GOD

Two is joy. In creation everything is created in only two. Even the sprouting bud comes in twos. Sun and moon, day and night, two ears, two nostrils, two eyes, two cheers, two legs, two hands, two lungs, two hearts make one love. Two breasts for a single child. Two ovaries for a single uterus, two cheeks for a single face. And Two was God split into when he wanted to make Love

God made love to Himself
And a baby, baby, baby was born...

i know how to mew like a cat
i know how to talk like a babe
i know how to walk like elephant
i know how to sleep like a panda
i know how to laugh like a buffalo
and sing at the top of my stupid voice
i love to lay upon the roadside grass
and watch the moon till she landslides
warm up secrets i know, mimicry of babies
baba black sheep rhymes i know
and i love water paintings to draw
and chewing your hands, I know.

Love is not mine, neither is love yours. You cannot possess it, you cannot dispossess it. Every pure mind is permeable to love that flows through it, like water that runs across when there are no dams. Like rivers that flow through forests and wilds, love just flows through hearts when there is no barrier

ASIFA BANO FORGIVES

And five days later
Asifa's body they found
Torn and ravaged
Behind the bushes.

She was a "chirping bird"
was this Asifa girl
who ran like a deer
when they traveled,
she looked after the herd
sheep and cattle of all
That made her the darling
of the community" they said
She was the very centre
of our universe, they said.

My heart cries for her
for my little sister Asifa
for she is an angel girl
among the purest of angels
in the abode of Lord God
who is beyond all religions.

(Editor's Note :- Asifa was a Kashmiri girl, who was violated and murdered by miscreants. Although Antony has written about victims in many different countries, the poems have a predominantly Kashmir connection. Hemangi Sharma was born and brought up in Kashmir.)

BABY LOVE

love is ageing
yeah,
the babe
with blushes
gurgling with laughter
cooing with lust
is now ageing;

as a child
it crawled
under the bedsheet
pissed off
wetting the bedcovers
all its desires
and delicate harmones

when it grew up
it was naughty
doing all monkey tricks
licking at the wrong ends
and kissing at
gasping hens
and peeping into sucking thighs

now it is fine
young man
mellowed with
warmth of life
bustling with memories sweet
funny with kids afeet
and papaed he reasons

as days pass by
chicks flew
hips grew
hugging is paining
limbs are waning
energy elapsing
oozing fantasy
drying up

aged love
speaks in silence
a few words
break the air
mostly they in looks hide
brooding thoughts
meet eye to eye
the older couples
telepathise
searching meaning
in solemn strides.

Editor's Note :- Hormone spelt as "harmone" is deliberate. It is typical of Hemangi
Sharma's poetic style and liberty with language.

BABY MOTHERLESS

Today
motherless
I wonder
what I missed
the way she fed
balls and balls of rice
with ghee and dhal
the smell of mother
her Jasmine flower
the grace of her voice
her cheering moods
the way she played
with my silly toys
just enjoyed
with my age
a child she was
when I was
an adult she grew
up with me
she opened the sky
and showed me the stars
filled my nights
with fullness of moons
she preserved to me
the poem of life
the love of living
faith in healing
with delicate things
she was a wonder
for her weapons were modest
smiling in sadness

teaching life is in living
suckling throughout
was I her oozing energies
she stood for me
I made her a Child
and she mothered me
and I stood
with my babe
My mother inside me....

WHO WILL WOMB THE INNOCENT

Think of the children
running away from death
the little hearts
born to bombs
Penguins massacred
a child of tender forms
kissing the edge of Arms
if it is your baby
aged two or three
scorched by Sun
and Bleeded by the Sons
Sons of the Soil
are they???
Not one, but lakhs
every lakh has lakh hearts
and Crore emotions
Insecurities surmounted
refugee in own land
Begging for survival
Who will womb
Who will pouch the innocents?
World is sleeping
Ignoring the blood bath
when hearts are bruised
and hunted and hounded
Death Play, Smell of Death
stinking cruelty
Why the world is Quiet
the dead ones are no ones
the wounded, the limbless
the bleeding

Terrorists are littered
by Terrorist Attacks
When love fails
Hatred Survives
When Houses shatter
Whore Houses are born.......
BABIES ARE SOLD
Mother is sleeping
her babies are sold
for prices cheap;
bedded to aged sacks;
to seed them weeds,
her kids are raped
bloomed newly
her kids are kid supplies
when schooling shakes
mothers are sleeping
when fathers are bedding
When the nudists betray
purity and decencies
models bare
remaining formalities
animals display
mothers are for Nature
Human mothers
babying at night
and sleeping at light.

Editor's Note :- The use of typical Indian words like Lakh (hundred thousand) and Crore (ten million) in such poems betrays Antony Theodore's identity as the Indian mystic Hemangi Sharma. This poem has not been edited.

BIRTH OF A CHILD

A poem is born
when a child is born;

the little love,
it's tender tale

soft fingers
cracking voice
closed looks

hugging bulk
a tiny sack
of tender emotions

its urge to suckle
the milking spots
hunger is inborn?

in silence
when the urge is over
a sleeping verse

shut in dreams
beyond the closed eyes
lies all wonders;
about to bud and blossom

the lovely noises
and squeals of delight
it utters in coming days
the lovely turn arounds

first hug so tight
warmth exuding
the bond of heavenly taste

the way it looks
the new world around
with new ideas brimming
and novelties swimming

the day it crawls
sucking own limbs and legs
twisting and turning and
clinging and climbing

sizing things
with inner dimensions
stuffing all hand
into the little mouth

dancing in the leaking rain
pouring from puzzling drain

the languages it speak
with its silent looks

little chuckles
and telling muses
every baby blossoms
with thousands of poems within
soon to be manned
with dry prose stained.

GOD REINCARNATES

Man reproduces
God reincarnates

seeds germinates
souls transmigrates

what is in a Sperm?
what is in a Spirit?

Babies cry for food
Babies cry for love
Lust hankers for nest
Zest harbours rest.

When life is midway
have you started anyway?
When we are midlife
our kids ask us why us?

Every thought reincarnates consciousness
Every matter reincarnates energy sources
when man rapes, weeded out are orphans
when gods escape, churned out are seasons

who made passions
and then mansions?
who scaled Oceans
and then confusions?

Man reproduces
God reproduces toooooooooo

Every being
unto his own liking
Every being
multiplies its own looking

Man seeds to litter kids
God designs for better ends
What we dearly desire
he provokes to sire
his own children
made of charms and auras

when out of raw ovum
moulds of plastic mud
a finished clay form
inside woman delivers
frames of expanding energies

when the diving sperm connects
links of God signals
for his reincarnations
does he tool man's passions?

Are we gods abnormal?
Super Gods reigning Invisible
Are we Pronouns?
Nouns encased in mediums undecipherable?

Humans are we puppets?
handled by unfathomable Cosmics
Are we all bakable Ceramics
potteries filled up to Eternity's Quest...?

A BABY CRIES

the baby cries
with a single syllable
you wonder upto skies
and offer all things and lies

you offer pen
it asks to write
you write on palm
it wants to lips

you offer a flower
it shrieks for more
by the time you add
it swallows down the bud

you show the moon
if it is not noon
it looks down to earth
and wants it to come to path...

you whistle to distract
it cries for mews of a cat
if you become an elephant
it kicks you at horse speed

all tired, when you are done
then you realise the play
the child was crying for attention
nothing in focus, only added attention.....

MOTHER OF A SCHOOL GOING SON

Once a mother
went to the school
of her school going son
who made her a fool
for she loved him
and lived for him
he was to her
everything from sun to flower

all the classmates
came to greet
the mother of the boy
and giggled and laughed
for the mother had only an eye
and her face was cartoon like

in the evening
when the boy reddening
came home angrily
and chided his mum
never again come to my school
or else I will quit going to school
Mother was so sad
and agreed every word
and from that day on
her feet never touched
the grounds of her son's school

the son grew up
but the scar never healed
it hurt him so

to have a one eyed mother
he wanted to go
far off to shake off
this shame of his life
to have a mother without an eye

he went away
to a place far off
where he got a job
a wife and a kid
and had his last laugh
when once the mother
wished to see
the little infant
her milking tottler
she planned to visit
and visit did she
to be turned away
by the unforgiving son
rudely stung and stray

days and months passed
and life rolled on away
but days of the mother
gathered no more further
the son was soon sent a word
by neighbours attending the mad
by the time the son arrived
the mother's body was engraved
and there she lay the one-eye woman
in peace of heaven and ease of mind

a word or two and the son was handed
a letter from the dead mum lastily penned
he tore it open as he was on his way
back to his home as nothing did it worry
to say goodbye to things he have not cared
the letter carried a message
the dead mother had written
to the babe of her womb
who all life and flesh did her tomb
"dear son, the eyes of yours
are the eyes of mine
when in the sunshine
of my youth did you meet
an accident and lost your sight
I gave you my looks
to cheer up your looks
so that the world outside
didn't say things bad and blind
not you be and handsome find
though dead I see through you
you are now my only eyes
and I see the world truly
through you and your eyes only..."

that was the story of the one-eyed mother
who weighed upon the sobbing future
of her insolent and selfish son.

THE CHILD BRIDE

She can't handle it
her body is too soft
and fragile to bear the thrust
of brutal assaults
into her innocent virginity
yet to become a virgin
she is but only a child
and that too devoid of hormones
required of a bride
her delicate body
and more delicate mind
her tender emotions
and her more tender passions
are all crucified
in the one Cross
and he who bled for the innocents
his one drop of blood he shed
for her the bleeding bride.....

even before she was out
of naked emotions
she was made naked
on her bridal bed
her purity of mission
lost in blatant vulgarity
for a preying beast
cannot be more cruel
than the chivalrous lord
of a childhood bride.

INFANT GOD TRAPPED IN SCHOOL

when the little one in infancy
came out of mother's womb
it cried in cold and insecurity
hunger started hugging it tight

some body hold me close
some body give me milk
some body clothe me warm
some body make me yours

the new born being's wish was granted
god incarnated as mother, grandmother
then it opened it's eyes and saw the world
focussing on things multiplying into untold

colour images it saw from its inward eyes
lovely things of past and previous births
giggling with mirth at midnight sleeps
it started laughing with no cause to treat

now god appeared in forms of life
blue sky, bubbles and birds that fly
mewing cats and the minute ants
green leaves and glowing petals

to touch was the next urge of the kid
and god came as spoons and toys
water pools, ladders and watery falls
mounting soil bed and hilling earth cups

and when the child grew up still
he went to school and found nothing
the teachers were all beating
and the books were all boring
aching he prayed before sleeping

Oh God! Come to my school on gentle toes
lest my teacher put you to teaching chores
and play with me with amusing wonders
hush! invisible and intelligent games we gather
to fool the madam and feed hours sweeter.

PUPPY'S LOVE

Across the hectic road
jumped up a puppy boy
wagging her tail of torment
stood a helpless mother
watching her plunge

The road was full and so mighty scary
dangerous for even humans who hurry
tongue he waved to his mother in worry
and took the ferry to motherhood deary

Those who watched it all stood still
for love on earth so thoughtless never fill
human kids think twice before they love
whether they gain or loose or life cease

It was an Act of God
and divine will be done
the angel of motherhood stepped in
and carried the puppy to mum's lap.

MONGOOSE MUM

baby cuddling
her little darlings
the mangoose mum
is caution's synonym

Love the beauty
that stands erect
with the soft paws
stern in the airy straws

the supple trunk
strokes your heart
the velvetty motion
is a sight of evolution

the alert looks
caution strewn books
every smell that itches
from far away hills

the most amazing sight
is the babies' flight
they find their ways beneath
the motherly umbrella heap

the mother's heart is largest
to the passing baby dearest
the melting eloquence
of a mother's care sings
as he traces her hunting bed
armouring her kids with her clueless spread.

BABY IN A LEAF

The language of nature
me too silly to nurture;
yet when leaves speak
I cant help, but squeak.

the palms of green
yellow, red and lean
their destiny veined
all art forms
spring from their dreams.

the colours of green
as I was amazed look on
an enormous leaf
my eyes fell upon
I stooped to kiss the grandma queen
what a large heart she was bestowed in vain.

red leaves, they kill me with their beauty
watch the liquidity of the texture aplenty
mellowed shine of depth rich in splendour
and the yellow beauty wise and intelligent
yellow leaves take you to life's very end.

leaves are the souls of our unborn babies
from earth they are carried by tree trunks to lullabies
till we take them in they fall not lovelies
sticking to the green mum they sing in breeze stories.

LITTLE ANGEL ASIFA

My little angel Asifa
We are all crying seeing
your dead body in the dust

the stones with which they struck you to death

after strangling your innocent throat

There is blood on Indian conscience.

In foreign nations
the great India
of ancient rishis
is known as a rape nation.

Is there no one to put an end to it?
Is there no one???

O mighty God where are you?

(Editor's Note :- Asifa was a Kashmiri girl, who was violated and murdered by miscreants. Although Antony has written about victims in many different countries, the poems have a predominantly Kashmir connection. Hemangi Sharma was born and brought up in Kashmir. She makes repeated references to Asifa in her poetry.)

AT MY MOTHER'S BREASTS

When I was a little baby
I looked at the breasts
Of my radiant mother
Round and lovely
Full of tasty milk

I longed to suck the milk of love
I longed to suck the milk of joy
I longed to suck the milk of playfulness
And she hugged to me her lovely breasts

This was the time I knew what was love
This was the time I knew motherly care
This was the time I knew that love is joy
And God told me so am I to you.

CHRIST AS A BABY

Intense is the relationship
between mother and child
Nine months carrying safe
in the womb with so much of love

This is like the relationship
with God and a human being
God loves us all like a loving Mother
Who cares and lives only for the baby

A mother suffers when the child suffers
Even a cough of the child gives her pain

When the child has to have an injection
She suffers with the child and feels the pain

Sometimes babies are taken away from mother
Babies are stolen and sold for their tiny organs
They amass wealth by killing and selling kidneys
and other body parts of simple and beautiful babies

Some use babies for medical research
Some use them for their carnal search
So cruel is this world and into this world
Christ comes as a Baby to save the Man.

HER CHILD WAS BRUTALLY MURDERED

Bruised, derided, cursed, defiled
she looked at her tender child
covered with bloody scourges

She kissed the wounds
cried bitterly spending tender tears
at the cruelties of the terrorists

The child died on her arms
She hugged the dead child
to her heaving breasts

O you Mother, my God
You are the fount of love!
Touch my spirit now

Help me to forgive the murderers
Of my child of love, my only one,
They killed my husband too

Now I am all alone
Counting the sands
of the burial ground
I look up begging God
to make this world
a place of mercy

God is for me, my mother
the Fountain of Love
Make my Heart One
with yours O Divine Mother.

Poet's Note :- I heard these words of suffering from a Christian woman who came as a refugee to Dortmund, Germany. Got inspired and wrote this. I was astonished to see the act of forgiveness in her words even when her husband and child were killed before her eyes and she raped. God works wonders in human hearts indeed.

In memory of all murdered children - I realized many of them never really had a cover photo (but who have either a birthday or angel day) :-

Tanisha Wilson, Jessica Reagin, Cyndi Faye Abell and 168 others :- November 19, 2014 at 5: 38 am

Willow Claxton :- November 20, 2014 at 6: 22 am

Sierra Lynn Newbold, Teigan Peters and Kelsey Smith-Briggs :- November 24, 2014 at 12: 46 am

Karlita Acosta Nuñez :- November 19, 2014 at 10: 54 pm

Paull Andersson and Kayleigh Jayne Slusher :- February 2, 2014 at 8: 17am

Mary Collins Dempsey : November 20, 2014 at 1:00

Editor's Note :- It is not clear when the poet Hemangi Sharma visited Dortmund, Germany. Is she talking of a past life in Germany? The names mentioned above have apparently been taken from social media like Facebook showing the dates of birth of murdered kids.

MOTHER OF STEVE JOBS

55 million aborted
Thousands die daily
What would they have become?

Steve job writes:

"My mother was only 23
When I was born in her womb

She went through a lot
to keep me alive

So many forced her
to abort me in her holy womb

She took a decision
to love me instead
to keep me in her womb

Come what may, she said
i will face it".

Here I am Steve Jobs.

PROTECT BABIES

Protect all Babies
they are full human beings
from the time they become
seeded in the womb
they all have life

Life is sacred
Life is a gift
from God to man
let it not waste
in a butcher's drain

come we shall all bow
before all the women
who take a decision
to keep the unborn
in their holy womb
and nurture them
till they are born
into a world
of love.

EVERY HUMAN NEEDS LOVE

Every human heart hungers for love

If you do not have the warmth
of God's love in your heart
there is no celebration
there is no joy

The world loves power and possession
You can be very successful in this world
You have every material thing in your life

But without a heart full of love
what is this life's worth?

It is simply nothing to cherish
nothing at all

Love, love, love
Give, give, give
Forget and forgive
That alone is the mantra
Of a life lived in love.

BE FRUITFUL AND MULTIPLY

Be fruitful and multiply,
was the command
given to Adam
and throughout
the Word of God
we find parents
bringing their children
to the Lord.

The Bible exhorts
parents to instruct
their children in the
things of God

to train them in
the way they should
go and to teach
them the Holy Scriptures,

which are able to
give them the wisdom
that leads to salvation,
through faith in
Christ Jesus our Lord.

Editor' Note :- Reference to Bible : "Be fruitful and multiple, and fill the earth and subdue it, and have dominion over all creation (Genesis 1.28). It has in Hindu scriptures : "After creating the progenitors through cosmic fire sacrifice, Prajapati exhorted them to multiply. (Gita 3.10).

CHRISTMAS BELLS ARE RINGING

Listen O birds and animals
Trees and flowers and leaves
Rivers and seas everywhere.
The Christmas Bells are ringing.

The old and familiar singing
on the streets this cold evening
They are sweet and they bring
our sweet childhood memories
when we sang with mummy dearest
lovely songs of love and mercy
and a new birth of Jesus Christ.

Now think of the millions of abortions
and the killing of innocent children
the abandoned and the homeless
the forced child labor of little ones
silently killing their lovely future
no smile, no school, no play, no joy
entire spring of their lives spent
toiling for the mighty and the rich.

Human beings, sing with the angels
"Let there be peace on this earth
and glory to God in the mighty heavens
Be of goodwill, spread smiles everywhere".

The belfries of all Christendom
ring out in an unbroken song:
"peace, peace, joy, joy everywhere
goodwill, goodwill for all men".

Let us sing together:
Sing it on our way, at dawn and dusk,
sublime chanting and dancing along
"peace on earth, for men
and for good willed women!"

Let all religions unite.
"We shall not kill in the name of God".

Bow your head and heart
and chant in your heart
"We shall not hate
We shall only love
And we shall spread
God's joy and peace"

The pealing of bells from the towers
I can hear loud, clear and deep.

God is not dead
God is not asleep
Peace shall prevail
Goodwill in the hearts
Of men and women
Shall reign till the end of times.

PART – IV

I AM YOUR BABY, MOM

IN DIFFERENT LANGUAGES

God knows the thoughts of all human beings even before they are released from their tongues. One who tunes into God knows all the thoughts welling up in all human hearts. One who loves God alone knows how to cross the language barrier. Such a one loves talking to God in silence.

Wherever life is, there is talking. Talking is the beauty of life link. Talk of feelings, talk of emotions, talk of not only words but heavenly responses to nature, wind, breeze, ocean, sky, birds and all. In silence body talks, in darkness inner light talks. At night the nocturnals talk. In peace hearts talk with love. In harmony music talks with symphonies. Talking without words is the most beautiful talking. Talking with dance, talking with lyrics, talking with memories, nostalgic. When you are old and alone, you talk to pictures of dead ones, to tombs of dead ones, to your beloved ones gone by. You talk to your own feelings, you talk to them who are in your consciousness. Talking is as enormous as your silent gifts of love.

Talk to God. Talk with your heart absorbed in God. Listen incessantly to God's silent talk. Do not underestimate the power of the Word. Do not forget that the pen is mightier than all the injustices that holy earth can contain.

ARABIC

by Houda Boukassoula

إنّني طفلك يا أمّاه
لم آت بمفردي يا أمّاه
نزلت ملائكة الرّحمان إلى رحمك
من السّماوات العلى نزلت
في رحمك الورع فيّا روحا نفخت
لم آت بمفردي يا أمّاه
هكذا أقدار الإله شاءت
كنت سعيدا وفي مغارة الحبّ نمت
في رحمك الورع
في سلام هناك نمت
الملائكة حرستني
ولي دعت
كي أكون دائما بسلام
حتّى أولد على وجه الأرض
أغان سماويّة للولادة ردّدت
كي تعزفها على قيثارتها الذّهبيّة يوم ولادتي
عندما كنت أنام في رحمك
كانت الملائكة تعودني
يا أمّي الحبيبة ولم تعلمي
كنت سعيدا أن أولد
وأكون لك أحبّ ولد
أردت أن أبتسم
أردت أن أغنّي

أردت أن ألعب
أردت أن أرضع حليب صدرك
حتّى أبلغ رضاك
وأرى إبتسامة على محيّاك
عندما أنهي كلّ الحليب من صدرك الحنون
في رحمك أمّاه بكلّ ذلك حلمت
ولكن في يوم قاس
قرّرت قتلي
الشّياطين في الجحيم بقرارك علمت
على أعلى الطّبول دقّت
ألحانا شيطانيّة عزفت

اجتمعت ثمّ جاءت
جاءت وعلى دوائر رقصت
رقصت و غنّت
على خطوط رقصت
على دوائر رقصت
على أصابع أقدامها رقصت
على رؤوسها رقصت
و أشرس الأغاني أنشدت
على طبول الشّيطان قرعت
كان الجحيم كله سعيدا
بقرارك قتلي

أتعلمين عندها كم أنا بكيت
أتعلمين عدد الملائكة الّتي بكت
أتعلمين أنّ السّماء كلّها بكت
يوم متّ في رحمك الورع
للحظة وقبل قتلي بوحشيّة
خلتني أرى عجز الإله القدير

ARABIC (Syrian)

By Mrs Shurouk Hammoud (Damascus)

أنا طفلك يا أمي

طفلك أنا.. يا أمي
لم آتِ وحدي يا أمي
حطّت ملائكة الله في رحمك
حلّقت من السموات العظيمة
ووضعتني في رحمك المقدس.
لم آت من تلقاء نفسي يا أمي
الله أراد ذلك.
كنت سعيداً للغاية في كهف الحب الجديد
في رحمك المقدس
ونمتُ بسلامٍ هناك
شاهدتني الملائكة
وصلّوا لأظلّ دائماً سالماً
حتى أولدَ على وجهِ الأرض
تمرّنوا على أغنيات الولادة السماوية
ليعزفوها على القيثارات الذهبية يوم ميلادي.
حين كنت نائماً في رحمك
كانت الملائكة تأتي إليّ
ولم تعرفي ذلك يا أمي الأغلى.
كنت سعيداً بولادتي
طفلاً حبيباً لك.
أردتُ أن أبتسم
أن أغني
أن ألعب

أن أرضع حليب صدرك
حتى ترضين.
أردت أن أرى ابتسامة وجهك
حين أرضع كل حليب صدرك المحب.
تلك كانت أحلامي وأنا في رحمك أمّاه.
لكن وفي يومٍ وحشيّ
قررتِ قتلي
سمعتِ الشياطين في الهاوية قرارك
جلبوا الطبل ذو الصوتِ الأعلى
وعزفوا إيقاعات الشيطان
اجتمعت الشياطينُ جميعها

أتت لترقص في دوائر
لتقفزَ وتغني
رقصوا ضمن صفوف
ضمن دوائر
على أصابع أقدامهم رقصوا
رقصوا على رؤوسهم
وغنّوا أعنفَ الأغنيات
وعزف قارعو طبول الشيطان
كانت جهنّم كلّها سعيدة
بقرارك أن تقتليني.
أتعلمينَ كم بكيت؟
أتعلمين كم من الملائكة قد بكت؟
أتعلمينَ كيف بكتِ السموات جميعاً
في يومِ مقتلي في رحمك المقدّس؟
في اللحة التي سبقت مقتلي بوحشية
رأيتُ الله القويّ يبكي عاجزاً

قصيدة للشاعر الألماني أنطوني تيودور
ترجمة الشاعرة السورية: شروق حمود

BENGALI

মা, মই তোমাৰ সন্তান- ডঃ এন্টনী থিয়ডোৰ

মা, মই তোমাৰ সন্তান
মই ইচ্ছা কৰি অহা নাছিলোঁ, মা
গৌৰৱময় স্বৰ্গৰ পৰা
ঈশ্বৰৰ দূতে তোমাৰ গৰ্ভলৈ প্ৰৱেশে কৰি
মোক থাপণ কৰিছিলি তাত

মই ইচ্ছা কৰি অহা নাছিলোঁ, মা
বিধিৰি ইচ্ছাত আহিছিলোঁ মই

তোমাৰ সুকোমল গৰ্ভত
প্ৰেমেৰ এটা নতুন ঠিকিনা পাই আনন্দতি হৈছিলোঁ
আৰু যাপন কৰিছিলোঁ সুখনদিৱা।
স্বৰ্গৰ দূতবোৰে মোক নবীক্ষণ কৰিছিলি
সহিঁতে মনিত কৰিছিলি যেনে
পৃথিৱীৰ মুখ নদেখো পৰ্যন্ত
মোক কুশলে ৰাখে

মই জন্মা দিনা সোনৰ বীনা বজাবলৈ
সহিঁতে জন্মোৎসৱত গোৱা গীতবোৰৰ আখৰা কৰিছিলি

মই তোমাৰ গৰ্ভত শুই থকা দিনিবোৰত
তোমাৰ অগোচৰে
স্বৰ্গীয় দূতবোৰে মোক দেখো কৰিছিলি

তোমাৰ প্ৰিয় সন্তান হৈ জন্মিবিলৈ
মোৰ যে কিমান হেপাঁহ আছিলি

মোৰ হাঁহিবিলৈ হেপোঁহ আছিলি
ইচ্ছা আছিলি গান গাবলৈ
খেলিবিলৈ ইচ্ছা আছিলি মোৰ
ইচ্ছা আছিলি তোমাৰ স্তনযুগলৰ অমৃত পান কৰিবিলৈ
চাব বিছাৰিছিলোঁ তোমাৰ দুগ্ধ পান কৰাৰ সময়ত

নগিৰা অহা তোমাৰ মুখৰ হাঁহি

গৰ্ভত থকা কালত দেখো মোৰ সপোন আছিলি এয়া, মা

কিন্তু এটা দুৰ্ভগীয়া দিনি আহিলি
যেতিয়া তুমি মোক মাৰি পেলোৱাৰ কথা ভাৱিলা

যাতনাৰ দূতবোৰে তোমাৰ সেই মনৰ আলচ
কান পাতি শুনিলে
আসুৰকি আনন্দৰে নৰকৰ দূতবোৰে
দুল কোবাই কোৰাই
গাবলৈ ধৰিলে নষ্ঠিৰোৱতম সুৰ-
জঁপিয়াই জণপিয়াই
মোক আগুৰাই আগুৰাই
শাৰী পতি পাতি গাইছিলি
ঘুৰি ঘুৰি নাচিছিলি
ভৰিৰ আঙুলিতি ভৰ দি নাচিছিলি
মূৰতো ভৰ দি নাচিছিলি সহিঁত
সহিঁতে ফুৰ্তিতি দুল বজাই নাচিছিলি
তুমি যে মোক মাৰি পেলোব খুজিছা তাক জানি
নৰকৰ পূৰ্ন ৰাজ্যই আনন্দ গান কৰিছিলি।

মোৰ হয়িা ভগা ক্ৰন্দন জানো তুমি শুনা পাইছিলা?
পৰিত্ৰ দূতবোৰৰ কান্দোন জানো তুমি গম পাইছিলা?
তোমাৰ পৰিত্ৰ গৰ্ভত মোৰ কৰুন মৃত্যু দেখো
সমগ্ৰ স্বৰ্গবাসীৰ ক্ৰন্দন জানো তুমি জানিব পাৰিলা?

মোক নিৰ্দয়ভাবে মাৰি পেলোৱাৰ আগে আগে
মই দেখো পালো সৰ্বোপৰিজিনাৰ অসহায় কান্দোন!

BIKOL Language (Philippines)

By Ms Abegail Kyla Bilan (Goa, Philippines)

Ako an saemong aki, Nay.
Na bakong hale sa sadiri kong Ina.
Mga anghel kan Diyos an nagdara
Sa sinapupunan hale sa kalangitan
Asin binuhay sa saemong tolak.

Bakong hale sa sadiri kong Ina;
Ginusto ini kan Bathala

Sobra an kaogmahan
Sa bag-ong kweba kan pagpadangat,
Igdi sa saemong tolak
Nagtuturog nin trangkilo.
Hinihiling kan mga anghel.
Habang nangangadyi
Na ako pirming isalbar
Sa pagkapangaki igdi sa daga.

Nag-eensayo nin mga kantaon
Makalangit, sa sakong pagdatong.

Habang turog sa saemong tolak
Mga anghel, pirming nagbibisita
Dae mo aram, padaba kong Ina.

Maogma kutang ipangaki
Mamatean man kota

Gusto kong magngirit
Gusto kong mag-kanta
Gusto kong magkawat
Gusto kong magmimi saemo
Hanggang sa ika maogma.
Gusto kong mahiling an saemong mgga ngirit
Habang nagmimimi saemo.

Ini man sana an sakong mga pangarap, Nay.

Kudi sa sarong maraot na aldaw
Naisip mong gadanon ako.

Nadangog ka kan mga demonyo.
Tolos na dinara an pagkakusog kusog na tambol
Tuminogtog nin maka-demonyo.
Gabos sinda, nagkasararo,
Nagraranihan, nagsarayawan, paikot-ikot,
Luminukso asin kuminanta.
Nagsarayaw sinda nin nakapila.
Nagsarayaw sinda nin paikot.
Nagsarayaw sinda sa saendang mga bitis.
Nagsarayaw sinda sa saendang mga payo.
Kuminanta nin pagkakusog kusog na mga kantaon,
Mga demonyong nagtatambol
Maogmahon an buong impiyerno,
Na pinili mong gadanon ako.

Aram mo baya kun gurano ako naghibi?
Aram mo baya kun gurano naghibi an mga anghel?
Aram mo baya kun gurano nagluksa an buong kalangitan
Sa aldaw kan sakong kagadanan
Sa saemong sinapupunan?

Asin sa sarong hidali bag-o ako nawara,
Nahiling ko an makaherakon na paghibi kan Bathala.

DUTCH (Netherlandish)

by Sylvia Frances Chan

Ik Ben Jouw Baby, Mamma

Ik ben je baby, Mama

ik ben je baby, Mama
ik ben niet naar mijn eigen moeder gekomen
Gods engelen vlogen naar je baarmoeder
van de machtige hemel
en plaatsten mij in jouw heilige schoot

ik ben niet naar mijn eigen moeder gekomen,
God wilde het zo.

ik was zo blij in mijn nieuwe grot van liefde,
in je heilige baarmoeder
en sliep daar vredig
de Engelen keken toe
ze baden
om me in alle tijden veilig te houden
totdat ik op de aarde geboren zal worden

ze oefenden hemelse geboorte-liederen
om te spelen op hun gouden harpen op mijn verjaardag

toen ik in je baarmoeder sliep
kwamen de Engelen naar mij toe
je wist het niet, mijn lieve moeder
ik was blij om geboren te worden
als je geliefde kind

ik wilde glimlachen
ik wilde zingen
ik wilde spelen

ik wilde je moedermelk opzuigen
tot je tevreden was.
ik wilde de glimlach op je gezicht zien
wanneer ik al je melk van je liefhebbende borsten
opgezogen heb

dat waren mijn dromen in je baarmoeder, Ma.

Maar op een wrede dag
heb je besloten me te vermoorden

De duivels in de Hades
hebben gehoord over uw beslissing
ze brachten de luidste trommel
gespeeld in de duivelse ritmes
alle duivels kwamen samen
kwamen en dansten in cirkels
springen en zingen
ze dansten in lijnen
ze dansten in cirkels
ze dansten op de tenen
ze dansten op hun hoofden
ze zongen de wildste nummers
en de duivelsdrummers speelden
de hele hel was blij
dat je hebt besloten me te vermoorden.

Weet je hoeveel ik huilde?
weet je hoeveel engelen huilden?
weet je hoe de hele hemel huilde
op mijn sterfdag in jouw heilige baarmoeder?

Een moment voordat ik wreed vermoord werd
zag ik de Almachtige God hulpeloos huilen.

FARSI

By Ghazal Ebrahimzade (Iran)

من از آن تو ام مادر

به خود نامده ام آخر

خداوند و سفیرانش از آن فردوس

والا قدر دمیدندم در جانت

و

..جا دادن به زهدانت

به خود نامده ام این من

که خواست ایزد این بوده است

ندانستی تو ای مادر

سفیران خداوندی مرا دیدند...زدند بر چنگ [فرزندی]

که بودش بسی زرین

که فرزندی به صلح و [ناز] خوابیده به زهدانی چنین تقدیس

سرود نور تابیدند و دمادم هم بودند ناظر

که پای من رسد بر فرش این گیتی

و من عاشق بودم شادان به غار کوچکم خندان

سفیران خداوندی بودند ناظر بر این دوران

دلم پرواز می خواهد که باشم طفل محبوبت

بخندم و بخوانم و کنم بازی

بنوشم شیره ی جانت

بیابم هم تو را راضی

در آن هنگام که جان بخشد به جانم شیره ی جانت

همین رویاست که خوابانده مرا در عمق زهدانت

...فغان

از صبح بی دادی

که قصد جان من کردی

تمام نسل دیو و دد

به سرزمین مرگ و درد

شنیدند نغمه ی رایت

و

آهیختند و آمیختند و

آویختند سرود بزم و

کوبیدند بر طبلی [سرد]

و چرخیدند و کوبیدند

به یک حلقه

به یک شاهراه

به روی پا

به روی سر

به وحشی ترین آوا
پریدند و سراییدن در یک خط و کوبیدند
به طبلی [بس گران و سرد]
تمام جهنم غرق شادی شد
که قصد جان من کردی
چه بی پایان گریستم من
چه بی پایان باریدند
فرشتگان و آسمان
که حتی آن دم آخر
کمی قبل از مرگ خون بارم

خداوند توانمد هم
به عجز و لابه می بارید.

by Aya Poetess

Ako'y Iyong Sanggol, Ina

Ako ang iyong sanggol, Ina.
Hindi ako nagmula sa iyong sinapupunan.
Ang mga anghel ng Diyos
bumaba mula sa kalangitan
at sa iyong sinapupuna'y ako'y inilaan.

Hindi ako nagmula sa aking Ina;
Ang Panginoong Diyos ang Siyang may nais.

Ako'y maligaya sa bagong yungib ng pagmamahal,
sa iyong banal na sinapupunan
at doon ako'y natulog ng mahimbing.
Ang mga anghel ang aking mga taga-bantay.
Sila'y nagsipagdarasal
para ako'y manatiling ligtas
hanggang ako'y maisilang sa mundong ibabaw.

Sila'y nagsipagsanay ng makaluwalhatiang awitin ng
kapanganakan
upang sa aking pagsilang kanila'y tugtugin ang ginintuang
harpa.

Habang ako'y nasa iyong sinapupunan
sila'y nagtungo sa akin.
Ito'y lingid sa iyong kaalaman, aking mahal na Ina.

Maligaya akong isinilang
Bilang iyong mahal na supling.

Nais kong ngumiti
Nais kong kumanta
Nais kong maglaro
Nais kong tumanggap ng gatas mula sa iyong dibdib

Hanggang sa ika'y makuntento.
Nais kong makita ang mga ngiti sa iyong mukha
Hanggang makuha ko ang lahat ng gatas mula sa iyong
mapagmahal na dibdib.

Ang mga ito'y panaginip ko mula sa iyong sinapupunan, aking Ina.

Ngunit sa isang malupit na araw
Naisipan mong ang buhay ko'y kitilin.

Ang mga diyablo sa Hades
Nadinig ang iyong nais.
Inilabas nila ang pinakamalakas na tambol,
at tinugtog ang maladiyablong ritmo.
Ang lahat ng mga diyablo ay nagsama-sama,
nagsipagdatingan at nagsipagsayawan,
nag-tatalunan at nag-aawitan.
Sa hana'y sila'y nagsipagsayawan.
Sa lupon sila'y nagsipag-indakan.
Nagsipag-indayog ang kanilang mga talampakan.
Nagsipag-indakan ang kanilang mga kauluhan
Maiilap na awiti'y kanilang hinimig
at ang tambol ng demonyo'y kanilang pinadinig.
Ang buong impyerno ay nagsipagdiwang
sa pasya mong ako'y paslangin.

Batid mo ba ang aking pagtangis?
Batid mo rin ba ang mga anghel ay nag-iiyakan din?
Batid mo ba ang sangkalangita'y nagluluksa
dahil sa aking pagyao sa iyong sinapupunan?

At bago ang sandaling ako'y malupit na pinaslang,
aking nasilaya'y Diyos na May-kapal kahabag-habag na lumuluha.

FILIPINO

By Nikho Schin Valle (Philippines)

Ako ay iyong anak ina.
Ako ay di nanggaling sa aking sariling ina.

Ang mga anghil ng Diyos lumipad pababa tungo sa iyong
sinapupunan
Galling sa makapangyarihang kalangitan
At nilagay ako sa iyong banal na sinapupunan.

Di ako nanggaling sa aking sariling ina
Ginusto ito ng diyos.

Ako ay masaya sa aking bagong kuweba ng pagmamahal,
Sa iyong banal na sinapupunan.
At ako'y natulog doon ng mapayapa.
Nanuod ang mga anghel.
Sila ay nagdasal
Para ako'y palaging ligtas
Hanggang sa ako'y isilang sa balat ng lupa

Nagsanay sila ng makalangit na kanta para sa pagsilang
Para tumugtog ng mga gintong alpa sa aking kaarawan.

Ng ako'y natutulog sa iyong sinapupunan
Ang mga anghel ay pumupunta sa akin.
Di mo lang ito alam, aking pinakamamahal na ina.

Masaya ako na ako'y pinanganak
Bilang iyong pinakamamahal na anak.

Ginusto kung ngumiti
Ginusto kung kumanta
Ginusto kung maglaro
Ginusto kung sumuso sa iyo upang mainom ang gatas sa iyong
suso
Hanggang sa ikaw ay kuntento na.
Ginusto kung Makita ang ngiti sa iyong mukha
Habang sinisipsip ko ang gatas mula sa iyong mapagmahal na

suso.

Yan ang aking pangarap sa loob ng iyong sinapupunan, ina.

Ngunit sa isang malupit na araw
Pinili mong kitilin ang aking buhay.

Ang mga demonyo sa impyerno
Ay nadinig ang desisyon.
Dinala nila ang pinaka maingay na tambol,
Tumugtog ng mala-demonyong indayog.
Ang lahat ng mga demonyo ay nagtipon,
Nagtipon at sumayaw ng pabilog,
Habang tumatalon at kumakanta.
Sumayaw sila ng naka hanay.
Sumayaw sila ng pabilog.
Sumayaw sila gamit ang kanilang paa.
Sumayaw sila gamit ang kanilang mga ulo.
Kinanta nila ang pinaka mabangis na kanta
At tumugtog ang mga demonyong tambulero.

Ang buong impyerno ay masaya
Na pinili mong ako ay patayin.

Alam mo ba kung gaano ako umiyak?
Alam mo ba kung ilang anghel ang umiyak?
Alam mo bang ang buong kalangitan ay umiyak
Ng araw na ako'y namatay sa iyong banal na sinapupunan?

Sa mga sandali bago ako'y malupit na pinatay
Nakita ko ang makapangyarihang Diyos na umiiyak at walang
magawa.

FRENCH

By Tapan Kumar Pradhan

Je Suis Ton Bébé, Maman

Je suis ton bébé, Maman
Je ne suis pas venu de ma volonté, Maman
Les anges de Dieu sont descendu
Des cieux hauts and puissants
Et m'ont placé dans ton vontre sacré

Je ne suis pas venu de ma volonté, Maman
Plûtot Dieu le voulait comme ça

J'étais si heureux
Dans ma nouvelle caverne d'amour
Dans ton vontre sacré
Que j'y ai dormi dans la joie
Les anges m'ont regardé et ont prié
Pour me garder toujours en sécurité
Jusqu'à ce que je naisse sur la surface de la terre
Ils ont pratiqué des chants célestes de naissance
Pour jouer de leurs harpes dorées a mà naissance

Quand je dormais dans ton ventre en paix
Les anges des cieux hauts venaient à moi
Mais tu n'etais pas au courant de cette, Maman

J'étais heureux d'être né
comme ton enfant bien aimé

Je voulais sourire
Je voulais chanter
Je volais jouer

Je voulais sucer le lait de tes seins
Jusqu'à ce que tu sois complètement satisfait
Je voulais voir le sourire sur ton visage
Quand j'ai sucé tout ton lait de tes seins aimants

C'étaient mes rêves dans ton ventre, Maman

Mais un jour sombre et cruel est venu
Où tu as décidé de m'enlever ma vie

Les diables du Hadès ont entendu
Parler de ta terrible décision, Maman
Ils sont sorti leurs tambours les plus forts
Et les ont joués dans des rythmes diaboliques
Tous les diables sont sortis ensemble
Et ils ont dansé en cercles
Sautant et chantant ils dansaient en lignes
Ils dansaient en rond
Ils dansaient sur les orteils
Ils dansaient sur leurs têtes
Ils ont chanté les chansons les plus folles
Et les batteurs diaboliques ont joué
Tout l'enfer était heureux
Que tu aies decidé de me tuer

Sais-tu Maman combien j'ai pleuré?
Sais-tu combien d'anges ont pleuré?
Comment tout le ciel a pleuré ce jour-là
Le jour de ma mort dans ton ventre sacré

Un moment avant d'être cruellement assassiné
J'ai vu le Dieu tout-puissant pleurer impuissant

GAELIC (Irish)

By Marie Shine (Ireland)

Is Mise Do Mhac Leanbh, A Mhammaí.

Is mise do mhac leanbh, A Mhammaí.
Níor tháinig mé ar mo mháthair féin.
Tháinig aingeal Dé le do bhroinn
ó na flaithis mighty
agus chuir mé i do bhroinn naofa.

Níor tháinig mé ar mo mháthair féin;
Bhí Dia ag iarraidh é sin a dhéanamh.

Bhí mé chomh sásta i mo uaimh nua grá,
i do bhroinn naofa
agus chod sé ansin síochánta.
D'amharc na h-uillinneacha.
D'ordaigh siad
a choinneáil sábháilte i gcónaí
till go rugfar mé ar aghaidh an domhain.

Chleachtaigh siad amhráin breithe neamhaí
a imirt ar a n-harpair órga ar mo lá breithe.

Nuair a bhí mé ag codladh i do bhroinn
D'úsáid na haingil teacht ormsa.
Ní raibh a fhios agat, mo mháthair dearest.

Bhí áthas orm a rugadh
mar do belovedchild.

Bhí mé ag gáire
Bhí mé ag canadh
Bhí mé ag iarraidh a imirt
Bhí mé ag iarraidh do bhainne cíche a tharraingt
Go dtí go raibh tú sásta.
Bhí mé ag iarraidh an aoibh gháire a fheiceáil ar d'aghaidh
Nuair a thógfaidh mé do bhainne ar fad ó do bhrollach grámhara.

Ba iad mo bhrionglóidí i do bhroinn, Mam.

Ach ar lá éadrócaireach
chinn tú a mharú.

Na diabhal sa Hades
chuala tú faoi do chinneadh.
Thug siad an druma is airde,
a bhí i rithim devilish.
Tháinig na diabhal go léir le chéile,
tháinig agus damhsa i gciorcail,
ag léim agus ag canadh.
Rince siad i línte.
Rinne siad i gciorcail.
Rinne siad damhsa ar na toes.
Rinne siad ar a gcinn.
Bhí siad ag canadh na n-amhrán is fírinne
agus imir na drumadóirí diabhal.
Bhí an ifreann ar fad sásta
gur chinn tú a mharú.

Tá a fhios agat cé mhéad a d'iarr mé?
Tá a fhios agat cé mhéad aingeal a chuaigh?
An bhfuil a fhios agat conas a chuaigh an neamh ar fad
ar mo lá bháis i do bhroinn naofa?

Nóiméad sula ndearnadh morgáiste cruaidh orm
Chonaic mé an Dia Uile-chumhachtach ag caoineadh go míchuí.

by Peter Tweer

Mama, ich bin dein Baby

Mama, ich bin dein Baby.
Ich bin nicht in meiner eigenen Mama herangewachsen.
Gottes Engel flogen
vom mächtigen Himmelreich zu dir
und legten mich
in deinen heiligen Leib.

Ich bin nicht in meiner eigenen Mutter herangewachsen;
Gott wollte es so.

Ich war so glücklich
in meiner neuen Höhle der Liebe,
in deinem heiligen Leib
und schlief dort friedlich.

Die Engel beobachteten mich.
Sie beteten,
um mich immer sicher zu bewahren,
bis ich auf Erden geboren werde.

Sie übten himmlische Geburtslieder ein,
um sie auf ihren goldenen Harfen zu meinem Geburtstag zu
spielen.

Als ich in deinem Bauch schlief,
kamen die Engel zu mir.
Das hast du nicht gewusst, meine liebste Mama.

Ich war glücklich, als dein geliebtes Kind
geboren zu werden.

Ich wollte lächeln.

Ich wollte singen.
Ich wollte spielen.
Ich wollte deine Muttermilch saugen,
bis du zufrieden warst.
Ich wollte das Lächeln auf deinem Gesicht sehen,
wenn ich deine ganze Milch
aus deinen liebenden Brüsten saugte.

So waren meine Träume in deinem Bauch, Mama.

Aber an einem mörderischen Tag
hast du beschlossen, mich zu töten.

Die Teufel in der Unterwelt
hatten von deiner Entscheidung gehört.
Sie brachten die lauteste Trommel
und spielten höllische Rhythmen.
Alle Teufel kamen zusammen
und tanzten in Kreisen,
springend und singend.
Sie tanzten in Reihen.
Sie tanzten im Kreis.
Sie tanzten auf den Zehen.
Sie tanzten auf ihren Köpfen.
Sie sangen die wildesten Lieder,
und die Teufelstrommler spielten.
Die ganze Hölle war glücklich,
dass du dich entschieden hattest, mich zu töten.

Weißt du, wie sehr ich geweint habe?
Weißt du, wie viele Engel weinten?
Weißt du, wie der ganze Himmel weinte
an meinem Todestag in deinem heiligen Leib?

Einen Moment, bevor ich grausam ermordet wurde,
sah ich sogar den Allmächtigen Gott hilflos weinen.

GREEK

By Ms Mary Skarpathiotaki

Είμαι το μωρό σου Μητέρα.
Δεν ήρθα από μόναχό μου, μαμά.
Οι άγγελοι του Θεού πέταξαν στη μήτρα σας
από τους ισχυρούς ουρανούς
και με έβαλε στην ιερή σας μήτρα.

Δεν ήρθα από μόναχό μου, μαμά.
Ο Θεός το ήθελε έτσι.

Ήμουν τόσο χαρούμενο στη νέα μου κοιλότητα αγάπης,
στην ιερή σας μήτρα
και κοιμόμουν εκεί ειρηνικά.
Οι γωνίες παρακολουθούσαν
Προσευχήθηκαν
να με κρατάς πάντα ασφαλές
μέχρι να γεννηθώ στο πρόσωπο της γης.

Εξασκήθηκαν με ουράνια τραγούδια γέννησης
να παίζω στις χρυσές άρπες τους την ημέρα των γενεθλίων μου.

Όταν κοιμόμουν στη μήτρα σου
Οι άγγελοι συνήθιζαν να ρχονται σε μένα.
Δεν το γνωρίζατε, αγαπητή μου μαμά.

Ήμουν χαρούμενος που γεννήθηκα
ως αγαπημένο σας παιδί.

Ήθελα να χαμογελάσω
Ήθελα να τραγουδήσω
Ήθελα να παίξω
Ήθελα να πιπιλίσω το μητρικό σας γάλα
Μέχρι να είστε ικανοποιημένοι
Ήθελα να δω το χαμόγελο στο πρόσωπό σας
Όταν ρουφώ όλο το γάλα σας από τα αγαπημένα στήθη.

Ήταν τα όνειρά μου στη μήτρα σας, μητέρα.

Αλλά σε μια σκληρή ημέρα

αποφασίσατε να με σκοτώσετε.

Οι διάβολοι στον Άδη
ακούσατε για την απόφασή σας.
Έφεραν το πιο δυνατό τύμπανο,
να παίξει στους πιο διαβολικούς ρυθμούς.
Κι όλοι οι διάβολοι συναντήθηκαν,
ήρθαν και χόρεψαν σε κύκλους,
χοροπηδώντας και τραγουδώντας
Χορεύαν σε γραμμές.
Χορεύαν σε κύκλους.
Χορεύαν στα δάκτυλα.
Χορεύαν στο κεφάλι τους.
Τραγούδησαν τα πιο αγριωπά τραγούδια
και οι διάβολοι ντράμερ έπαιζαν.
Όλη η κόλαση ήταν ευτυχισμένη
στην απόφασή σας να με σκοτώσετε.

Ξέρεις πόσο φώναξα
Ξέρεις πόσοι άγγελοι έκλαψαν
Ξέρετε πώς φώναξε ο Παράδεισος ολάκερος
την ημέρα της θανάτωσής μου στην ιερή σας μήτρα

Μια στιγμή πριν δολοφονηθώ σκληρά
Είδα τον παντοδύναμο Θεό να κλαίει απαρηγόρητα.
Δρ. Αντώνιος Θεοδώρης
I Am Your Baby Mum - Poem by Dr. Antony Theodore

by Kostas Lagos

Είμαι Το Μωρό Σου Μαμά

Είμαι το μωρό σου μαμά.
Δεν ήρθα μόνο μου μαμά.
Άγγελοι του Θεού πέταξαν μέχρι τη μήτρα σου
από τους ισχυρούς ουρανούς
και με εναπόθεσαν στην ιερή σου μήτρα.

Δεν ήρθα μόνο μου μαμά
Ο Θεός το θέλησε.

Ήμουν τόσο χαρούμενο στη νέα μου σπηλιά αγάπης,
στην ιερή σου μήτρα
και κοιμήθηκα εκεί ειρηνικά.
Οι άγγελοι φύλαγαν.
Προσεύχονταν
να είμαι πάντα ασφαλής
μέχρι που να γεννηθώ στο πρόσωπο της γης.

Πρόβαραν ουράνια τραγούδια γέννησης
για να τα παίξουν με τις χρυσές άρπες τους την ημέρα των
γενεθλίων μου.

Όταν κοιμόμουν στην κοιλιά σου
Οι άγγελοι έρχονταν σε μένα.
Εσύ δεν το ήξερες, αγαπημένη μου μαμά.

Ήμουν χαρούμενο που θα γεννηθώ
ως το αγαπημένο σου παιδί.

Ήθελα να χαμογελάσω
ήθελα να τραγουδήσω
ήθελα να παίξω
ήθελα να θηλάσω το μητρικό σου γάλα
μέχρι να ευχαριστηθείς.

Ήθελα να δω το χαμόγελο στο πρόσωπό σου
Όταν θα θήλαζα όλο το γάλα σου από το αγαπημένο στήθος σου.

Αυτά ήταν τα όνειρά μου στην κοιλιά σου, μαμά.

Αλλά μια σκληρή ημέρα
αποφάσισες να με σκοτώσεις.

Οι διάβολοι στον Άδη
έμαθαν την απόφασή σου.
Έφεραν το δυνατότερο τύμπανο,
έπαιξαν στους διαβολικούς ρυθμούς.
Όλοι οι διάβολοι μαζεύτηκαν,
ήρθαν και χόρεψαν σε κύκλους,
πηδώντας και τραγουδώντας.
Χόρευαν σε γραμμές.
Χόρευαν σε κύκλους.
Χόρευαν με τα δάχτυλα των ποδιών τους.
Χόρευαν με τα κεφάλια τους.
Τραγούδησαν το πιο άγρια τραγούδια
και οι διάβολοι τυμπανιστές έπαιξαν.
Ολόκληρη η κόλαση ήταν ευτυχής
που αποφάσισες να με σκοτώσεις.

Ξέρεις πόσο έκλαψα;
Ξέρεις πόσοι άγγελοι έκλαψαν;
Ξέρεις πώς όλος ο ουρανός έκλαψε
την ημέρα του θανάτου μου στην ιερή μήτρα σου;

Μια στιγμή πριν σκληρά δολοφονηθώ
είδα τον παντοδύναμο Θεό να κλαίει αβοήθητος.

HAUSA
Poem by Abdul Basit Ismail

Ni Danka Ne, Mum -
Ni ne jaririnku.
Ban zo kan mahaifiyata ba.
Mala'ikun Allah sun sauka zuwa ga mahaifinka
daga manyan sammai
kuma sanya ni a cikin mahaifa mai tsarki.

Ban zo kan kaina ba;
Allah yana son haka.

Na yi murna a cikin sabon kogo na kauna,
a cikin mahaifa mai tsarki
kuma barci a can cikin salama.
Harsuna suna kallo.
Sun yi addu'a
don kiyaye ni lafiya kullum
har sai da za a haife ni a fuskar ƙasa.

Suna yin waƙoƙin haihuwar samaniya
su yi wasa a kan harpinsu na zinariya a ranar haihuwata.

Lokacin da nake barci a cikin mahaifa
Mala'iku sun kasance sun zo gare ni.
Ba ku san shi ba, ɗana na ƙauna.

Na yi murna da za a haife ni
a matsayin ƙaunatacce.

Ina so in yi murmushi
Ina so in raira waƙa
Ina so in yi wasa
Ina so in shayar da nono madara
Har sai kun yarda.
Ina so in ga murmushi a fuska
Lokacin da na shayar da madararka duka daga ƙirjinka mai
ƙauna.

Su ne mafarkina a cikin mahaifa, Mum.

Amma a cikin mummunan rana
Ka yanke shawarar kashe ni.

Shaidan a cikin Hades
ji game da yanke shawara.
Suka kawo ƙarar murya,
buga a cikin rudun shaidan.
Dukan aljannu sun taru,
ya zo ya rawace a da'irori,
tsalle da kuma waƙa.
Suna rawa a cikin layi.
Suna rawa a cikin da'irori.
Suna rawa a kan yatsun kafa.
Suna rawa a kan kawunansu.
Suna raira waƙoƙi mafi kyau
kuma shaidan ya buga wasan.
Dukan jahannama yayi farin ciki
cewa ka yanke shawarar kashe ni.

Ka san nawa kuka?
Ka san yawan mala'iku da kuka?
Ka san yadda dukan sama ke kuka
A ranar da nake mutuwa a cikin tsattsarka mai tsarki?

Wani lokaci kafin an kashe ni da mummunan rauni
Na ga Allah Mai Iko Dukka yana kuka ba tare da wani taimako ba.

HINDI

by Ankit Raj Goyal

मैं तेरा बच्चा हूं माँ

मैं तेरा बच्चा हूँ माँ
मैं खुद से नहीं आया हूँ माँ
भगवान के फरिश्ते उड़ के आए थे कोक में तेरी
दूर मेहरबा जन्नत से कहीं
और चुपके से मुझे सौंप के चले गए थे कोक में तेरी

मैं खुद से नहीं आया हूँ माँ
भगवान की मर्जी का भेजा हुआ हूँ मैं माँ

मैं बहुत खुश था मेरे नए प्यार के पालने में
तेरी पाक कोक के झूले में
और सो रहा था वही, सुकून की लहरों में
फरिश्ते देख रहे थे
इबादत कर रहे थे
मेरी महफूतियत की
इस कायनात में मेरे जन्म की

वे पैदाइश के पाक नगमें गा रहे थे
मेरे मुबारक जन्म पर अपने सुनहरे बाजों पे बजाने को
जब मैं सोया हुआ था कोक में तेरी
फरिश्ते आते थे आहिस्ता से
मेरी प्यारी माँ, ये बात नहीं इल्म में तेरी
मैं खुश था पैदा होने को
तेरा प्यारा अजीज बच्चा बनने को

मैं हंसना चाहता था, गाना चाहता था
मैं खेलना चाहता था

तेरी छाती से दूध पीना चाहता था
जब तक तू खुश ना हो जाए
मैं तेरे चेहरे की मुस्कुराहट देखना चाहता था
जब मैं तेरी छाती से तेरा सारा दूध पी लूँ

तेरी कोक में वो मेरे सपने थे माँ
मगर उस जालिम दिन
तूने मुझे खत्म करने का फैसला कर लिया

हेडस के शैतानों को
तेरे फैसले की खबर लग गई
वो अपने सबसे तेज नगाड़े ले आए
अपनी शैतानी धुन में लगे बजाने
सारे शैतान इकट्ठे हो गए
और गोल गोल लगे नाचने
कूदते हुए गाते हुए वो कतारों में नाचे
वो गोलों में नाचे, वो पंजों पर नाचे

वो अपने सरों के बल नाचे
वो अपने जंगली गाने गा रहे थे
और नगाड़े ढोल बजा रहे थे
पूरी जहन्नुम खुश थी
कि तुम मेरी साँस रोक रही हो

तुम्हें पता है मैं कितना रोया था?
तुम्हें पता है फरिश्ते कितना रोए थे?
क्या तुम्हें पता है कि पूरी जन्नत कैसे रोई थी
तुम्हारी पाक कोक में मेरी मौत के दिन?

उस आखिरी लम्हें में, मेरी दर्दनाक हत्या से पेहले
मैंने खुद सबसे ताकतवर भगवान को रोते देखा, बेसहारा अकेले

HINDI

By Tapan Kumar Pradhan

मैं तेरा बच्चा हूँ मां

मैं तेरा बच्चा हूँ माँ
अपनी मर्जी से मैं आया नहीं था माँ
खुदा के फरिश्ते ले आए थे मुझे स्वर्ग से
और डाल दिये थे मुझे तेरी कोख में

अपनी मर्जी से मैं आया नहीं था माँ
खुदा की मर्जी से ही मैं आया था माँ

कितना खुश था मैं अपनी प्रेम की गूफ़ा में
पवित्र प्यार की तेरी उस कोख में
सोया रहता था मैं सुकून से वहीं
फरिश्तों ने देखा, और इबादत की खुदा से
कि मैं सलामत रहूँ सदा वहीं
जब तक कि धरती के पृष्ठ पर पैर न थाम लूँ

सुनहरी वीणा पर रियाज कर रहे थे वे रोज नगमें
बजाने के लिए मेरे जन्मदिन पर अनोखे दिव्य संगीत

जब मैं सोया रहता था प्यारी कोख में तेरी
स्वर्ग के ये फरिश्ते आते रहते थे मेरे पास
पर यह बातें नहीं थी जानकारी में माँ तेरी

मैं तो खुश ही खुश था इस जन्म के लिए
तेरा बच्चा बन कर माँ यहाँ आने के लिए

मैं तो हँसना चाहता था, गाना चाहता था
खेलना चाहता था
पीना चाहता था दूध तेरी छाती से माँ
देखना चाहता था आँखों में तेरी भरी मुस्कान
जबतक तेरी छाती से सारा दूध न पीता जाऊँ

यही तो थे सपने मेरे माँ तेरी कोख में

पर ऐसा भी एक निष्ठुर दिन आया
जब तूने फैसला कर लिया मुझे मारने को

यम लोक के शैतानों ने सुन लिया तेरा फैसला
और निकाल लिया तुरंत अपने ढ़ोल नगाड़े
सारे शैतान हो गए इक्कठ्ठे, झूमने लगे
शैतानी धुन में ज़ोर ज़ोर बजाने लगे
कूद कर, चिल्ला कर नाचने लगे
कतारों में नाचे, वृताकार में नाचे
पंजों पर नाचे, सर के बल नाचे
जैसे खुश था पूरा यमलोक मुझे मारने का
तेरे उस मनहूस फैसले से

जानती हो माँ कितना रोया था मैं उस दिन ?
जानती हो कितने सारे फरिश्ते रोये उस दिन ?
जानती हो सारा स्वर्ग लोक रोया था उस दिन
तेरी कोख में माँ मेरी मौत हुई थी जिस दिन

दर्दनाक उस मौत के आखिरी लमहों में देखा मैंने
महावली खुदा भी रो रहे थे मेरी उस दशा से
बेसहारा महसूस कर खुद को, यूं बिलकुल अकेले ।

MALAYALAM

By Parameswaran Nair Damodaran Nair

AMMAYUDE KUNJALLE NJAN ?

Njan ningalude kunju, Mamayan
Njan ende ishtaprakaaram ivide vannittilla
Daivattinde dootanmaar enne svargattil ninn paratti
Ninde vishuddha garbha paatrattil enne akki

Njan ende ishtaprakaaram ivide vannittilla
Daivattin idu inganeyaariunnu

Ende pranayattinde guhayil njan valare santushtanaayirunnu
Njan avide samaadhaanamayi kitannu
Dootanmaar enne nireekshikkukayum
Enikkuvendi praarthikkukayum ceytu
Angane njan bhum varunnatuvare surakshitanayi tutarum

Avar tangalude svarna kinnarattil svarggiya ganangal alapichu
Janmattil bhoomiyile ende varavinaayi paataan

Njan ningalude garbha paatrattinullil urangumpol
Svargattil ninnulla dootanmaar ende atukkal varumaayirunnu
Pakshe ende priyappetta ammayekkuricch ningal arinjirunnilla

Ningalude priyappetta kuttiyaayijanicchatil
njan santushtanaayirunnu

Enikku punchirikkaan aagrahamuntaayirunnu
Enikku paadanum kalikkaanum aagrahicchu
Ningalude mulakalil ninn paal kutikkan aagrahicchu
Ningal poornamaayum santrupta raakunnatuvare

Ningalude snehamulla mulakalil ninn njan ella paalum kutikkumpol
Ningalude mukhattu punchiri kaanaan njan aagrahicchu

Iva ende garbha paatrattinullile
ende svapnangal aayirunnu, amma

Pakshe, krooramaaya oru divasam
Ningal enne kollaan teerumaanicchu

Ningalude teerumaanattekkuricch narakattile pishachukkal kettu
Avar tangalude ucchattilulla kaittaalangal purappetuvicchu
Pishachinde taalattil kalikkukayum cheytu
Ella pisaachukkalum ottuchernnu
Avar vannu vrruttangalil nrruttam cheytu
Chaadukayum paadukayum avar varikalil nrruttam cheytu
Vrruttangalil nrruttam cheytu
Kaalviralil nrruttam cheytu
Avarude talayil nrruttam cheytu
Avar erravum paadukal paadi
Pisaach kaittaalakkaar avarude kaittaalangal vaayichu
Narakam muluvan santoshavaanaayi
Ningal enne kollaan teerumaanicchatil

Njan etramaatram karannjuvenn ningalkkariyaamo?
Etra dootanmaar karannjuvenn ningalkkariyaamo?
Aa divasam aakaasham muluvan karannjataayi
Ninde vishuddha garbha paatrattil ende maranadivasam

Enne krooramaayi kolappeduttunatin
Oru nimisham mumpu njan kondu
Sarvva shaktanaaya daivam nissahaayatayode karayunnat.

ODIA

by Bharati Nayak

ମୁଁ ତୋ'ର ସନ୍ତାନ ମା'

- - - - - - - - - - - - - -

ହେ ମୋର ଗର୍ଭ ଧାରିଣୀ ମା
ମୁଁ ତୋର ସନ୍ତାନ ମା
ମୁଁ ଏଠାକୁ ସ୍ୱଇଚ୍ଛାରେ ଆସିନଥିଲି ମା
ଈଶ୍ୱରଙ୍କ ଆଜ୍ଞାରେ ମୁଁ ତୋ ଗର୍ଭକୁ ଆସିଥିଲି

ତୋ ମମତାମୟୀ ଗର୍ଭରେ
ମୁଁ ଆନନ୍ଦରେ ଖେଳୁଥିଲି
ଆଉ ଶାନ୍ତିରେ ଶୋଇ ପଡୁଥିଲି
ମୋ ନିରାପଦ ପୃଥିବୀ ଅବତରଣ ନିମନ୍ତେ
ଦେବଦୂତ ମାନେ ପ୍ରାର୍ଥନା କରୁଥିଲେ
ଆଉ ମୋତେ ଜଗି ରହିଥିଲେ
ସେମାନେ ସ୍ୱର୍ଗୀୟ ବୀଣାରେ
ମୋର ଜନ୍ମ ପାଇଁ ଆଗମନୀ ସଙ୍ଗୀତ ପ୍ରସ୍ତୁତ କରୁଥିଲେ ।

ମୁଁ ତୋ ଗର୍ଭରେ ନିରାପଦରେ ଶୋଇପଡିଥିବାବେଲେ
ଦେବଦୂତ ମାନେ ତୋ ଅଜାଣତରେ ମୋ ନିକଟକୁ ଆସୁଥିଲେ
ହେ ମୋର ଅତି ପ୍ରିୟ ମା
ତୁ କି ଜାଣୁ
କେତେ ଅଧୀର ଆନନ୍ଦର ଆବେଗରେ
ତୋର ସନ୍ତାନ ହୋଇ
ଜନ୍ମ ନେବା ପାଇଁ ମୁଁ ଚାହିଁ ବସିଥିଲି ।

ମୁଁ ଚାହୁଁଥିଲି ମୁଁ ହସିବି ଗାଇବି ଖେଳିବି
ତୋ ଛାତିରୁ ଅମୃତ ପାନ କରିବାବେଲେ
ତୋ ମୁହଁରେ ଖେଳୁଥିବ
ସ୍ତନ ଦାତ୍ରୀ ମାତାର ସ୍ୱର୍ଗୀୟ ଆନନ୍ଦର ଅନୁଭୂତି
ତୋ ମୁହଁରେ ସେଇ ଆନନ୍ଦର ଝଲକ ଦେଖିବାକୁ
ମୁଁ ତୋ ଗର୍ଭରେ ଅପେକ୍ଷା କରିଥିଲି ।

କିନ୍ତୁ ମା'
କେଉଁ ଏକ ନିଷ୍ଠୁର ନିୟତିର ଖେଳରେ
ଦିନେ ତୁ
ମୋତେ ମାରି ଦେବାକୁ ନିଷ୍ପତ୍ତି ନେଲୁ ।
ନର୍କର ରାକ୍ଷସ ମାନେ
ବୋଧହୁଏ ତୋର ନିଷ୍ପତ୍ତି ଶୁଣିପାରିଥିଲେ
ଦୁନ୍ଦୁଭିର ନାଦରେ ମତ୍ତ ହୋଇ
ପାଇଶାଚିକ ଗାନ ଗାଇ
ସମୂହ ଉନ୍ମାଦର ନୃତ୍ୟ କରିଥିଲେ
ସେମାନେ ନାଚୁଥିଲେ ବୃତ୍ତାକାରରେ
କେତେବେଳେ ଧାଡି ହୋଇ
କେତେବେଳେ ପାଦ ଟିପରେ
କେତେବେଳେ ଶିରରେ ଭରା ଦେଇ
ସେମାନେ ଗାଉଥିଲେ ଆଉ ନାଚୁଥିଲେ ।

ଆହା ତୋ ନିଷ୍ପତ୍ତିରେ
ସେମାନେ କେତେ ଖୁସି ଥିଲେ
ସାରା ନର୍କ ରାଜ୍ୟ କେତେ ଖୁସି ଥିଲା
ଜାଣୁ ମାଁ ସେଦିନ କେତେ ମୁଁ କାନ୍ଦିଛି
ଦେବଦୂତ ମାନେ କେତେ ଲୁହ ଝରାଇଛନ୍ତି
ସାରା ସ୍ୱର୍ଗ କେତେ ଅଶ୍ରୁପାତ କରିଛି
ଯେତେବେଳେ ତୋ ଗର୍ଭରେ
ନିଷ୍ଠୁର ଭାବରେ ମୋତେ ମାରି ଦିଆଗଲା
ତାର ଟିକକ ପୂର୍ବରୁ ମୁଁ ଦେଖିଲି
ସର୍ବଶକ୍ତିମାନ ଈଶ୍ୱର ମଧ
ଅଶ୍ରୁ ଝରାଉଥିଲେ ।

ODIA

By Tapan Kumar Pradhan

ମୁଁ ତୋ'ର ସନ୍ତାନ ମା'

ମୁଁ ତୋ'ର ସନ୍ତାନ ମା
ମୋ ଇଚ୍ଛାରେ ମୁଁ ଆସି ନଥିଲି ମା

ସ୍ୱର୍ଗରୁ ଦେବଦୂତ ମାନେ ନେଇଆସିଥିଲେ ମୋତେ
ଆଉ ରଖିଦେଇଥିଲେ ମୋତେ ତୋର ପବିତ୍ର ଗର୍ଭରେ

ମୋ ଇଚ୍ଛାରେ ମୁଁ ଆସିନଥିଲି ମା
ଭଗବାନଙ୍କର ଇଚ୍ଛାରେ ଆସିଲି

କେତେ ଆନନ୍ଦରେ ରହିଥିଲି
ମୁଁ ମୋର ପ୍ରେମର ଗୁଣ୍ଠାରେ
ତୋର ପବିତ୍ର ଗର୍ଭରେ
ଶୋଇଥିଲି କେଡେ ଶାନ୍ତିରେ
ଦେବଦୂତମାନେ ଦେଖୁଥିଲେ ମୋତେ
ଆଉ ପ୍ରାର୍ଥନା କରୁଥିଲେ ଈଶ୍ୱରଙ୍କୁ
ନିରାପଦରେ ରଖିବାକୁ ମୋତେ
ପାଦ ମୋର ମାଟିରେ ନ ପଡିବା ଯାଏ

ତୋଳୁଥିଲେ ଝଙ୍କାର ସୁନାର ସ୍ୱର୍ଗୀୟ ବୀଣାରେ
ଗାଇବାକୁ ମୋ ଜନ୍ମଦିନର ଆଗମନୀ ସଙ୍ଗୀତ

ଶୋଇଥିଲି ଯେତେବେଳେ ମୁଁ ତୋରି ଗର୍ଭରେ
ଦେବଦୂତମାନେ ଆସୁଥିଲେ ନିତି ମୋ ପାଖେ
ତୋ ଅଜଣାରେ ମା', ତୋ'ର ଅଜଣାରେ

ମୁଁ ତ ଖୁସି ଥିଲି ଜନ୍ମ ହେବାକୁ
ତୋର ସ୍ନେହର ଶିଶୁ ରୂପରେ

ମୁଁ ଚାହୁଁଥିଲି ହସିବାକୁ
ମୁଁ ଚାହୁଁଥିଲି ଗାଇବାକୁ
ମୁଁ ଚାହୁଁଥିଲି ଖେଳିବାକୁ
ପିଇ ଯିବାକୁ ତୋର ବକ୍ଷରୁ କ୍ଷୀର, ମା
ତୋର ମନ ଶାନ୍ତି ନ ହେଲା ଯାଏ
ଦେଖିବାକୁ ଚାହୁଁ ଥିଲି ତୋ ମୁହଁରେ ଫୁଟିଲା ହସ
ତୋର ବକ୍ଷରୁ ସାରା କ୍ଷୀର ମୁଁ ଚୁଷି ନ ନେବା ଯାଏ

ଏଇ ତ ଥିଲା ସ୍ୱପ୍ନ ସବୁ ମୋର ମା' ତୋ ଗର୍ଭରେ

କିନ୍ତୁ ହଠାତ ଆସିଲା ଏମିତି ଏକ ନିଷ୍ଠୁର ଦିନ
ତୁ ନିଷ୍ପତ୍ତି ନେଇନେଲୁ ମୋତେ ମାରି ଦେବାକୁ

ନର୍କର ରାକ୍ଷସମାନେ ଶୁଣିଲେ ନିଷ୍ପତ୍ତି ତୋର
ଘେନି ଆସିଲେ ତାଙ୍କର ଢୋଲ ବାଦ୍ୟ ମାଦଳ
ବିକଟାଳ ରଡି କରି ପଇଶାଚିକ ତାଳରେ
ସବୁଯାକ ରାକ୍ଷସ ଆସି ଏକାଠି ନୃତ୍ୟ କଲେ
ବୃତ୍ତାକାରରେ ଢୋଲର ତାଳରେ ତାଳରେ
କେବେ ସରଳ ରେଖାରେ, କେବେ ଗୋଲାକାରେ
ନାଚିଲେ ମୁଣ୍ଡରେ, ପୁଣି ନାଚିଲେ ଆଙ୍ଗୁଲି ଟିପରେ
ଗାଇଲେ ଚିତ୍କାର କରି ବିକଟାଳ ନାଦରେ
ସାରା ନର୍କ ରାଜ୍ୟ ପୁରା ଖୁସି ଥିଲା ଯେମିତି
ମୋତେ ମାରିଦେବାକୁ ତୋର ସେଇ ନିଷ୍ଠୁର ନିଷ୍ପତ୍ତିରେ

ଜାଣିଛୁ ତୁ ମା, ସେଦିନ କେତେ ମୁଁ କାନ୍ଦିଲି
ଦେବଦୂତ ମାନେ ସବୁ କାନ୍ଦିଲେ କେତେ
ଜାଣିଛୁ ସାରା ସ୍ୱର୍ଗ କାନ୍ଦି ଉଠିଲା ସେଦିନ
ତୋ ପବିତ୍ର ଗର୍ଭରେ ମୋର ମୃତ୍ୟୁ ହେଲା ଯେଦିନ

ନିର୍ଘୃଣ ମୃତ୍ୟୁର କ୍ଷଣିକ ପୂର୍ବରୁ ମୁଁ ଦେଖିଲି
ସର୍ବଶକ୍ତିମାନ ଭଗବାନ ବି କାନ୍ଦୁଥିଲେ
କେମିତି ଏକ ଅସହାୟ ମୁଦ୍ରାରେ ।

PERSIAN

by Farzad Jahanbani

من نی نی کوچولوی توئم مامانی

من نی نی [کوچولوِ] توئم مامانی
خودم نخواستم که بیام مامانی ؛
فرشته های خدا، گذاشتنم توو بطنت
از بالای آسمونا [اومدم]
قرار من شده این بطن پاکت

خودم نخواستم که بیام مامانی ؛
خدا خواسته که من بیام [مامانی]

،من خیلی خوشحال بودم
توو خونه ی عشق جدید؛ توو بطن پاکت بودم
خوابیده بودم، کاملا آروم
فرشته ها رو من همش می دیدم
که دائما هستن واسم دعاخون
،تاکه بیام به دنیا
روی زمین [زیبا]

واسه سرود، تولدم مشغول تمرین بودن
برای اجراش [همه] چنگ طلا می زدن

وقتی که من می خوابیدم داخل بطن پاکت
فرشته ها می خواستن که همراه من باشن
ولی تو اینو نمی دونی اصلا، عزیزترینم ؛ مامانِ [خوب]ـم

من [دیگه] خیلی شاد بودم
که سوگولی و بچتم

من لبخند رو می خواستم
من آواز رو می خواستم
من بازی رو می خواستم
من میک زدن شیر رو، از وجودت می خواستم

.تا که تو راضی باشی
می خواستم ببینم لبخند ر و روو چهرت
وقت مکیدن شیر، از وجود پرمهرت
اینها بودن رویاهام
توو بطن تو مامانی

اما توو اون روز بی رحم
.تو خواستی من رو بکشی

شیطونای جهنمی
تصمیم تو رو شنیدن

اونها همه آوردن، قوی ترینِ طبل ها
با سرعتی شیطونی، می نواختن به اون ها
همه ی اون شیطونا با هم دیگه اومدن
اومدن و رقصیدن با همدیگه دور هم
بالا می پریدن ، آوازا می خوندن
می رقصیدن توو یک خط
می رقصدن دور هم
پا انگشتی می رقصیدن
روو سراشون می رقصیدن
وحشی ترین آهنگا رو می خوندن
به طبلای شیطونیشون می زدن.
اونا همه خوشحال بودن
از تصمیم تو
به کشتن من.

هیچ می دونی چقدر من گریه کردم؟
هیچ می دونی چند تا فرشته گریید؟
هیچ می دونی همه ی عرش گریید؟
اون روزی که من مردم داخل بطن پاکت؟

یه لحظه قبل قتل من با این ظلم
دیدم قوی ترین رو؛ من خدارو
که گریه می کرد بی امان[از این ظلم]

ترجمه موزون و نگارش به صورت ترانه اثر #فرزادجهانبانی از شعر :

by Gurleen Kaur Narang

ਮੈਂ ਤੇਰਾ ਜਾਯਾ ਹਾਂ ਮਾਂ

ਮੈਂ ਤੁਹਾਡਾ ਬੱਚਾ ਹਾਂ ਮਾਂ
ਮੈਂ ਆਪਣੀ ਮਰਜ਼ੀ ਨਾਲ ਨਹੀਂ ਆਇਆ.
ਪਰਮੇਸ਼ਰ ਦੇ ਦੂਤ
ਸ਼ਕਤੀਸ਼ਾਲੀ ਆਕਾਸ਼ ਤੋਂ
ਤੁਹਾਡੇ ਗਰਭ ਵਿਚ ਆਏ
ਅਤੇ ਮੈਨੂੰ ਤੁਹਾਡੇ ਪਵਿੱਤਰ ਗਰਭ ਵਿੱਚ ਰੱਖ ਦਿੱਤਾ.

ਮੈਂ ਆਪਣੀ ਮਰਜ਼ੀ ਨਾਲ ਤਾਂ ਨਹੀਂ ਆਇਆ;
ਰੱਬ ਚਾਹੁੰਦਾ ਸੀ ਕਿ ਇਹ ਹੋਵੇ.

ਮੈਂ ਆਪਣੀ ਨਵੀਂ ਗੁਫਾ
ਤੁਹਾਡੇ ਪਵਿੱਤਰ ਗਰਭ ਵਿਚ ਬਹੁਤ ਖੁਸ਼ ਹਾਂ
ਅਤੇ ਸ਼ਾਂਤੀ ਨਾਲ ਉੱਥੇ ਸੁੱਤਾ
ਫਰਿਸ਼ਤੇ ਏਿਹ ਦੇਖਦੇ ਤੇ
ਉਹ ਪ੍ਰਾਰਥਨਾ ਕਰਦੇ
ਮੈਨੂੰ ਹਮੇਸ਼ਾਂ ਸੁਰੱਖਿਅਤ ਰੱਖਣ ਲਈ
ਜਦ ਤੱਕ ਮੈਂ ਧਰਤੀ ਦੇ ਚਿਹਰੇ ਤੇ
ਪੈਰ ਨਹੀਂ ਰੱਖ ਲੈਂਦਾ.

ਉਹ ਜਨਮ ਦੇ ਸਵਰਗੀ ਗੀਤ ਅਭਿਆਸ ਕਰਦੇ ਹਨ
ਮੇਰੇ ਜਨਮ ਦਿਨ 'ਤੇ ਉਨ੍ਹਾਂ ਦੇ ਸੁਨਹਿਰੀ ਰੱਸਿਆਂ ਨਾਲ ਖੇਡਣ ਲਈ.

ਜਦੋਂ ਮੈਂ ਤੁਹਾਡੇ ਗਰਭ ਵਿੱਚ ਸੌਂ ਰਿਹਾ ਸੀ
ਦੂਤ ਮੇਰੇ ਕੋਲ ਆਉਂਦੇ ਸਨ
ਤੁਹਾਨੂੰ ਨਹੀਂ ਨਾ ਪਤਾ ਸੀ, ਮੇਰੀ ਪਿਆਰੀ ਮਾਂ!

ਮੈਂ ਜਨਮ ਲੈ ਕੇ ਖੁਸ਼ ਸੀ,
ਏਿਕ ਪਿਆਰੇ ਬੱਚੇ ਦੇ ਰੂਪ ਵਿੱਚ!

ਮੈਂ ਮੁਸਕਰਾਹਟ ਚਾਹੁੰਦਾ ਸੀ
ਮੈਂ ਗਾਉਣਾ ਚਾਹੁੰਦਾ ਸੀ
ਮੈਂ ਖੇਡਣਾ ਚਾਹੁੰਦਾ ਸੀ
ਮੈਂ ਤੁਹਾਡੇ ਦੁੱਧ ਨੂੰ ਚੁੰਘਣਾ ਚਾਹੁੰਦਾ ਸੀ
ਮੈਂ ਤੁਹਾਨੂੰ ਬਸ ਸੰਤੁਸ਼ਟ ਦੇਖਣਾ ਚਾਹੁੰਦਾ ਸੀ
ਮੈਂ ਤਾਂ ਤੁਹਾਡੇ ਚਿਹਰੇ 'ਤੇ ਮੁਸਕਰਾਹਟ ਵੇਖਣਾ ਚਾਹੁੰਦਾ ਸੀ.

ਇਹ ਤੁਹਾਡੀ ਕੁੱਖ ਵਿੱਚ ਮੇਰੇ ਸੁਪਨੇ ਸਨ, ਮਾਂ!

ਪਰ ਇੱਕ ਬੇਰਹਿਮ ਦਿਨ,
ਤੁਸੀਂ ਮੈਨੂੰ ਮਾਰਨ ਦਾ ਫ਼ੈਸਲਾ ਕਰ ਲਿਆ.

'ਹੇਡੀਜ਼' ਵਿਚਲੇ ਭੂਤਾਂ
ਜਦ ਤੁਹਾਡੇ ਫ਼ੈਸਲੇ ਬਾਰੇ ਸੁਣਿਆ
ਓਹ ਸਭ ਤੋਂ ਉੱਚਾ ਨਗਾੜਾ ਲੈ ਆਏ,
ਸ਼ੈਤਾਨ ਦੀ ਲਾਲੀ ਵਿੱਚ ਖੇਡਿਆ
ਸਾਰੇ ਸ਼ੈਤਾਨ ਇਕੱਠੇ ਹੋ ਗਏ,
ਅਤੇ ਵਿਚ ਨੱਚਣ ਲੱਗੇ
ਟਪਣਾ ਅਤੇ ਗਾਉਣਾ ਸ਼ੁਰੂ ਕੀਤਾ
ਓਹ ਕਤਾਰ ਵਿਚ ਨਚਦੇ ਸਨ
ਓਹ ਚੱਕਰਾਂ ਵਿਚ ਨਚਦੇ ਸਨ
ਉਨ੍ਹਾਂ ਨੇ ਉਂਗਲਾਂ 'ਤੇ ਨੱਚਿਆ
ਉਨ੍ਹਾਂ ਨੇ ਆਪਣੇ ਸਿਰ 'ਤੇ ਡਾਂਸ ਕੀਤਾ.
ਉਨ੍ਹਾਂ ਨੇ ਸਭ ਗਾਣੇ ਗਾਏ
ਅਤੇ ਸ਼ੈਤਾਨ ਢਾਡੀਂਡਰ ਖੇਡੇ
ਸਾਰਾ ਨਰਕ ਖੁਸ਼ ਸੀ
ਕਿ ਤੁਸੀਂ ਮੈਨੂੰ ਮਾਰਨ ਦਾ ਫ਼ੈਸਲਾ ਲਿਆ ਹੈ.

ਤੁਸੀਂ ਜਾਣਦੇ ਹੋ ਮੈਂ ਕਿੰਨਾ ਚੀਕਿਆ?
ਤੁਸੀਂ ਜਾਣਦੇ ਹੋ ਕਿ ਫਰਿਸ਼ਤੇ ਕਿੰਨਾ ਚੀਕੇ?
ਕੀ ਤੁਹਾਨੂੰ ਪਤਾ ਹੈ ਕਿ ਸਾਰਾ ਆਕਾਸ਼ ਕਿਵੇਂ ਰੋਇਆ
ਤੁਹਾਡੇ ਪੇਟ ਦੀ ਕੁੱਖ ਵਿੱਚ ਮੇਰੀ ਮੌਤ ਦੇ ਦਿਨ ਤੇ?

ਮੈਨੂੰ ਬੇਰਹਿਮੀ ਨਾਲ ਕਤਲ ਕਰਨ ਤੋਂ ਇੱਕ ਪਲ ਅੱਗੇ
ਮੈਂ ਸਰਬ-ਸ਼ਕਤੀਮਾਨ ਪਰਮੇਸ਼ਰ ਨੂੰ ਬੇਵੱਸੀ ਰੋਦਾ ਦੇਖਿਆ.

RUSSIAN

by Ekaterina M. Polischuk

Я твой ребенок, мама.

Я твой ребенок, мама.
Моя душа не сама вошла в тебя.
Ангелы прилетели с небес
И впустили меня в тою святую утробу.
Моя душа не сама вошла в тебя,
Так захотел Бог.
Я был так счастлив в своей новой пещере любви,
В твоей святой утробе,
Где я мирно спал.
И ангелы за мной наблюдали.
Они молились обо мне,
чтобы со мной ничего не случилось,
И я появился на этой земле.
Они практиковались в пении
И готовили свои золотые арфы,
Чтобы возликовать в день моего рождения.

Когда я спал в твоей утробе,
Ангелы приходили ко мне,
Ты ведь ничего не знала об этом, моя дорогая мама.
Я был счастлив от того, что стану твоим любимым сыном.
Я хотел смеяться,
Я хотел петь.
Я хотел играть.
Я хотел вкушать твое молоко,
Чтобы ты была довольна мной.
Я хотел видеть улыбку на твоем лице,
Когда ты кормишь меня молоком из своей груди.
Это были мои мечты, мама, когда я находился в твоей утробе.

Но однажды ты решила убить меня…
И демоны преисподней услышали об этом.

Они взяли свои громкие барабаны

И начали отстукивать свой дьявольский ритм.
Все демоны собрались вместе
И пустились в круговой пляс,
Прыгая и напевая свою ужасные песнопения.
Они танцевали в одной линии.
Они танцевали по кругу.
Они танцевали на ногах.
Они танцевали на головах.
Они пели свои ужасные песнопения,
И дьявольский барабанщик играл -
Все в аду были счастливы,
Так как ты решила убить меня.
Знаешь ли ты, как тогда я страдал?
Знаешь ли ты, как тогда оплакивали меня ангелы?
Знаешь ли ты, как оплакивали меня небеса
в день моей смерти в твоей святой утробе?

Мгновение назад я был жестоко убит…
Я увидел Всемогущего Бога,
беспомощно плачущего над моей душой.

By Christopher

Yo soy tu bebé mamá:

Yo soy tu bebé mamá.
No vine por mi cuenta mamá.
Los ángeles del Cielo bajaron a tu vientre
y me colocaron en tu santo vientre.

Yo no vine por mi cuenta mamá
Así lo quizo Dios.

Era tan feliz en mi nueva cueva de amor,
en tu santo vientre
y en paz ahí dormí.
Los ángeles me miraban.
Ellos rezaban
para tenerme siempre a salvo
hasta que naciera en la faz de la Tierra
Practicaron con esmero canciones de natividad
para tocar sus doradas harpas en mi nacimiento.

Cuando dormía en tu vientre
los ángeles venían a mí.
Tú no lo sabías, querida Madre.

Estaba tan feliz por nacer
y tu amado hijo por fín ser.

Quería sonreír
Quería cantar
Quería jugar
Quería tomar tu leche materna
hasta que tú estés satisfecha
Quería ver la sonriza en tu rostro
Cuando haya tomado toda la leche de tus amados senos.
Esos eran mis sueños en tu vientre Mamá.

Pero en un cruel día

decidiste matarme.

Los demonios del Hades
escucharon tu decisión.
El más sonoro tambor consigo trajeron,
y sus satánicos ritmos tocaron.

Todos los demonios se reunieron,
danzando en círculos vinieron,
cantando y saltando.
Haciendo filas danzaron,
haciendo círculos danzaron.
Sobres las puntas de sus pies danzaron
Sobre sus malvandas cabezas danzaron
Las canciones más salvajes cantaron
y los malditos tamborileros sus tambores tocaron.
Todo el infierno se alegró
Que habías decidido matarme.

Tienes idea cuanto lloré?
Tienes idea cuanto los ángeles lloraron?
Tienes idea cuanto el Cielo lloró?
El día de mi muerte en tu santo vientre.

En el instante antes de mi cruel asesinato,
vi al Dios Todopoderoso, impotentemente llorando.

by Juana Cruz

Yo soy tu bebe, mami.

Yo soy tu bebe, mami.
Yo no decidí venir al mundo, mami.
Los ángeles bajaron del cielo y
Me depositaron en tu vientre sagrado.

Yo no pedí nacer, mami.
Dios lo quiso así.

Estaba feliz en mi nueva cueva de amor
En tu vientre sagrado
Y allí dormí en paz.
Los ángeles velaban
Y oraban
Para mantenerme siempre seguro
Hasta el día que naciera en la tierra.

Practicaban canciones angélicas de nacimiento
En sus arpas doradas para mi cumpleaños.

Mientras yo dormía en tu vientre
Los ángeles venían a verme.
Tu no lo sabias, mi querida mami.

Yo esperaba feliz,
Nacer como tu querido bebe.

Yo quise sonreír.
Yo quise cantar.
Yo quise jugar.
Yo quise mamar leche de tus senos
Hasta saciarme.
Yo quise ver una sonrisa en tu cara
Mientras yo me alimento
De tus amados senos.

Eran mis sueños en tu vientre, mami.

Pero un cruel día
Tú decidiste matarme.

Los demonios en el Infierno
Se enteraron de tu decisión.
Buscaron el tambor más alto
Tocaron sus ritmos más demoniacos
Todos los demonios juntos
Danzaron en círculos
Saltando y cantando
Bailaron en líneas
Bailaron en círculos
Bailaron en sus pies
Bailaron en sus cabezas
Cantaron las canciones más salvajes
Y los demonios tocaron.
Todo el Infierno estaba feliz
Que decidiste matarme.

¿Sabes cuánto llore?
¿Sabes cuanto lloraron los angeles?
¿Sabes que todo el cielo lloro
En el día de mi muerte en tu sagrado vientre?
Un momento antes de que yo fuera cruelmente asesinado
Yo vi a Dios todopoderoso llorar inconsolable.

by Ojok Isaac

Aya, An Abedo Atini

Aya, an abedo atini.
Aya, pe obedo miti na.
Malaika a Jokamalo otwar iyi awura ni
Oyaa iker me polo
Te keta iyi awura ni acil.

Aya, pe obedo miti na;
Jokamalo omito kito.

Nu cunya yom iyi adake me mar,
Iyi awura ni acil
ate butu ikuc.
Malaikae ogwoka
Gin olego
Me wek abed akoma yot
Naka onywala i lobo

Gin opwonyo wer me nywale ipolo
Me atuka kede adungu inino nywale na

I Kare ame nu anino iyi awura ni
Malaika nu maro bino bota
Yin pe ingeo, Aya me amara

Nu yia yom ni i nywala
Calo atini me amara

Nu amito nyero
Nu amito wer
Nu amito tuku
Nu amito doto caki
Naka ka oromi
Nu amito neno bwonyo i wangi

Ka adoto cak kori me amara

Aya, manu nu leko na iyi awura ni

Ento inino arac
Yin imoko tami me neka

Jogi me kapiny
Owinyo gini tami
Ote kelo gini bul adit
Ote goyo gini kede dwon me jok
Jogi ducu obino karacel,
Obino te gure gini te myel
Te pyee kede wer
Gin omyelo ling
Ogure gini te myel
Gin omyeli iwi lwet gi
Gin omyelo iwii gi
Gin owero wer arac aloo
Eka jogi te goyo bul
Kapiny duc nu opong ilelo
Ni imoko tami me neka

Ingeo kit ame akok kede?
Ingeo malaika adii okok?
Ingeo kit ame polo aluto okok kede
Inino ame atoo iyi awura ni?

Ikare ame nu pwod pe atoo
Aneno Jokamalo won twer tye akok.

TAGALOG

by Diane Montemayor

I Am Your Baby Mum

Ako ang iyong sanggol, aking Ina.

Ako ang iyong sanggol, aking ina, , ,
hindi ako naparito dahil lang sa aking kagustuhan, , ,
Isang anghel ng Diyos ay bumaba sa iyong sinapupunan, ,
sa makapangyarihan langit, , ,
at inilagay ako sa iyong banal na bahay-bata.

hindi ako naparito sa aking sarili, aking ina, , ,
Ito ay kagustuhan ng Dios na lumikha.

Ako ay a masaya sa aking bagong pag-ibig buhat sa iyo, , ,
sa iyong banal na sinapupunan, , ,
at ako ay natutulog nang mapayapa, , ,
Ang mga angel ay nanalangin, , ,
upang panatilihing ako ligtas sa iyong sinapupunan, , ,
hanggang ako ay ipananganak sa ibabaw ng lupa.

Ang mga anghel sa kalangitan ay umaawit ng kagalakan sa aking
pagdating,
upang ipagdiwang sa kanilang, ang aking pagsilang…

Kapag ako ay natutulog sa iyong bahay-bata, ,
Ang mga anghel ay pumarito upang ako ay bantayan, , ,
hindi mo ba wari ito, ang aking pinakamamahal na ina

Ako ay masaya na ipinanganak, , , ,
bilang iyong minamahal na anak.

Nais kong ngumiti, , ,
Nais kong kumanta, , ,
Nais kong maglaro, , ,
Nais kong inumin ang gatas mula sa iyong pagmamahal
Nais kong makita ang ngiti sa iyong mukha

Ito ang aking mga pangarap sa iyong bahay-bata, aking ina, ,

Ngunit sa isang malupit na araw
ikaw ay nagpasya na kitilin ang aking buhay.

Ang mga masasama sa Hades
Naririnig ang tungkol sa iyong desisyon.
Kanilang dinala ang pinakamalalakas na trambolo, tumutugtog sa
malasamang tunog
Nagdiriwang at natutuwa sa iyong desisyon, , .
Ang lahat ng mga masasama ay nagtipon-tipon
Sumasayaw, , at habang nagagalak sa iyong ginawa,
Paglukso at pag-awit.
Sila ay sumasayaw na tila may guhit na sinusundan
Pumapalibot habang sumasayaw ng may kagalakan, , ,
Sumasayaw habang nakaluhod, , ,
Sumasayaw ng may kagalakan sa sarili, ,
At hindi maikubli ang kaligayahan nila, , ,
Sila ay umaawit sa pinakamasayang tono, malalakas, ,
sumisigaw, , , ,
Habang nilalaro ang timbolo ng trumpeta, , ,
Ang buong impiyerno ay humahalakhak, , , sa sobrang kasiyahan,
, ,
Ng magpasya ako ay iyong kitilin mula sa iyong sinapupunan.

Alam mo kung gaano ako sumisigaw?
Alam mo kung paano maraming mga anghel ay sumisigaw?
Alam mo ba kung paano ang buong langit ay umiiyak, , ,
sa aking araw ng kamatayan sa iyong banal na bahay-bata?

Ang isang sandal ng aking buhay, ako ay pinatay
Nakita ko ang Makapangyarihang Diyos umiiyak ng tuluyan.

by Marilou Madrazo

Ako'y Iyong Anak Inay

Ako'y iyong anak ina
Hindi ako pumaritong mag-isa
Pumanaog akong mga anghel sa langit ay kasama
At sa iyong sinapupunan ako'y maiging ipinunla
Hindi ako pumaritong mag-isa
Ito ay ginusto ng may likha.

Ako'y balot ng ligaya sa bagong kanlungan
Sa sagradong kuweba ng iyong sinapupunan
Natutulog ng mapayapa at matiwasay
Habang ang mga anghel sa akin ay nakabantay
Sabay-sabay na nananalangin
Hiling ay kaligtasan sa iyong piling.

Hangga't aking masilayan ang mukha ng daigdig
Awitin ng langit ay inihahandang isahimig
Kasabay ng tugtog ng ginintuang alpa
Upang sa'yo ay iparinig sa araw na itinakda
Habang nasa iyong sinapupunan nagpapahinga
Mga anghel paroot paritong bumibisita
Maging ito man ay lingid sa iyong kaalaman aking ina.

Ako ay sabik nang mailuwal
At maging anak na iyong pinakamamahal
Gusto kong ngumiti
Gusto kong kumanta
Gusto kong maglaro
Sumipsip mula sa iyong suso
Hanggang sa ako ay makuntento
Gusto kong masilayan ang iyong mga ngiti
Habang nakakanlong at ninanamnam ang gatas sa aking mga labi.
'Yan ang mga binuo kong pangarap

Na biglang naglaho nalang sa iisang iglap
Nang ang malupit na araw at dumating
At pinili mong sa iyong sinapupunan ako ay punitin.
Nay sa kaharian ng kasamaan ika'y narinig
Habang sinasambit mong ako ay ipapunit
Tila may piyesta, malalakas na tambol
Nakakabinging tugtugin nakakapangilabot!

At lahat ng demonyo ay nagtipon
Sumayaw ng pabilog
Kumanta, tumalon
Sumayaw sa iisang linya
Sumayaw ng pabilog
Sumayaw ang kanilang mga paa
Pati narin ang mga ulo nila
Kantang nakakabasag-tenga
Mga tambol na nagbabadya
Ang buong impyerno ay nagdiwang, nagpakabusog
Habang ang mura kong katawan ay pilit dinudurog.

Aking ina batid mo bang akoy lumuha?
Pati na mga anghel na aking kasama?
Ang buong kalangitan ay nagdalamhati
Nung araw sa loob ng sinapupunan ako ay iwinaksi
At bago pa man ang munting hininga ko'y binawi
Ang Diyos ay nasilayan ng may luha sa kanyang mga pisngi.

TAMIL
by Karunanidhy Shanmugam

நான்தான்..உன் சிசு

நான்தான்..உன் சிசு
அம்மா..
இங்கு உன் கருவறைக்கு
நானாக வரவில்லை
சொர்க்கத்தின் தேவதைகள்
ஏந்தி வந்து என்னை விடுத்து சென்றனர்
உன் கோவிலில்
ஆண்டவனின் சித்தம்
அதுவென்று..!
நானாக வரவில்லை!

அந்த தேவதைகள்
வேண்டியபடியே இருந்தன
உன்னுள் குடிகொண்ட நான்
பத்திரமாய் இருப்பதற்காக..
பத்ரிமாய் பிறப்பதற்காக..
நானும் மகிழ்ச்சியோடிருந்தேன்
முங்கியிருந்தேன் உன் கருவறை கடலில்

அவர்கள் யாழெடுத்து
தெய்வீக கணங்களை ஒத்திகை பார்த்தபடி
இருந்தார்கள்..
நான் பிறக்கும் நாளன்று இசைப்பதற்கென!
என்னை அவ்வப்போது வந்து
பார்த்தும் செல்வார்கள்
உன் கருவறையில் நான்
பள்ளி கொண்டிருக்கும் போது
அதனை நீ..அறிய மாட்டாய்
அம்மா..
உன் செல்லக் குழந்தையாய்

உலகினைத் தொட
நானும் காத்திருந்தேன் மகிழ்வோடு!

புன்னகை புரியவும்,
பாடவும், விளையாடவும்
நீ திருப்தியுறும் வரை
உன் பாலினை அருந்திடவும்
அதன் பின் உன் புன்னகையை கண்டிடவும்
கனாக் கண்டு கொண்டிருந்தேன்..
அம்மா!

கொடியதான நாளொன்றில்
என்னை கொல்ல
முடிவு செய்தாய்..
நரகத்தின் அரக்கர் கும்பல்
தாளமிட்டு நர்த்தனங்கள்
தலைகால் புரியாமல் ஆடி மகிழ
எம்பிக் குதித்து அவை சேர்ந்து பாட
மொத்த நரகமே விழாக்கோலம் பூண்டிட
என்னை கொல்லும் முடிவினை
நீ எடுத்தாய்!

எவ்வளவு நான் அரற்றினேன்
அழுது புரண்டேன்..
என்னோடு தேவதைகளும் கூட
அழுது தீர்த்தன..
சற்று முன்பாக
நீ என்னை கொன்ற போது
நான் கருவிலே கலைந்த போது
எல்லாம் வல்ல கடவுள் கூட
அழுது கொண்டிருக்கிறார்
செய்வதறியாமல்
உனக்கு தெரிகின்றதா..
..
அம்மா..?

TURKISH

By Metin şŞAHİN

DÜNYAYA GELMEDEN KATLEDİLEN - BEBEGİN FERYADI

ben senin sevgili yavrun..bebegin degil miydim ana...
bil ki ben kendğimden gelmedim sana
tanrının melekleri
taa ulvi göklerden kanatlarını açarak geldi yanına
ve o kutsal rahmişne yerleştirdi beni
ben sana kendiligimden gelmemiştim ana
bunu yüce tanrı istedi
çok mutluydum o sevgi dolu yeni sıgınagımda..yeni yerimde
o kutsal rahminde
orada...uyudum...mutlu ve hıuzurlu
melekler kolladı beni
dua ettiler bana
korumak için beni daima
yeryüzüne dogasıyadek
gelesiyedek

dogum günümde söylecekleri şarkıları tekrar ettiler
söylediler..cennetten getirdikleri
altın harblerinin eşliğinde söylecekleri

senin o kutsal rahminde ben uyurken
melekler swık sık ziyaret ederdi beni
sen bunun farkında degildin sevgili anam

dogacagım için çok mutluydum
senin sevgili çocugun olarak

gülmek isterdim
şarkı söylemek isterdim
oynamak isterdim
aglamak isterdim
göğüslerinden süt emmek isterdim
kana kana ... doyasıya
sen yeter deyinceyedek

o sevecen
göğüslerindeki bütün sütü tükettiğimde de
görmek isterdim yüzündeki mutlulugu...gülümsemeyi
senin rahmindeyken gördüğüm düşler...kurdugum hayaller buydu
ana

oysa o ugursuz...lanet günde
nasıl da karar verdin beni öldürmeye...katletmeye

cehennemdeki şeytanlar
duydu bu düşünceni
getiirdiler en kocaman..en gürültülü davullarını
şeytani danslarını oynadılar sevinçten
bütün şeytanlar toplandılar
birlikte halay çekerek oynadılar
halkalar..daireler halinde
şarkı söyleyip zıpladılar
sıralar halinde oynadılar
halkalar halinde oynadılar
ayuaklarının ucuna basarak oynadılar
taklalar atarak oynadılar başlarının üzerinde
en vahşi..en çılgın şarkılarını söylediler
davulları çalan şeytanlar da oynadı
bütün cehennem çılgına dönmüştü mutluluktan sevinçten
beni öldürmeye..katletmeye karar verdiğinden

benim ne kadar agladımı bilemesin
meleklerin de ne kadar agladığını bilemezsin ana
bütün evrenin de ne kadar agladığını da hiç bilemezsin
senin rahminde öldüğüm gün

vahşice öldürülmemden bir müddet önce
gördüm ki
beni o kutsal rahmine koyan yüce yaradanın bile gözlerinden yaş
geliyordu
yüce yaradan aglıyordu çaresizce

EPILOGUE

HEMANGI SHARMA

AS ANTONY THEODORE

I AM NOT FAKE

My dear poet friend
It is not a fake ID
Only my pseudonym
And I am not theoretical poet
I am a class one English poet
Though an unconventional poet
And an off the cuff instant poet
Name and fame I do not care
I am already published
In many languages
In many formats

Shakespeare was not dear
A follower like you poet
He was a poem in flow
You must have your own DNA
To become a poet of substance
I have been to a poetry academy
Where they stripped me nude
And now my poems they salute

HEMANGI SHARMA

AS DR ANTONY THEODORE

It was sometime in the year 2007 when I first noticed certain unusual activities in the internet during my browsing of spiritual topics. Social media posts by different persons with different IDs had the same underlying pattern and digital footprint. When I tried to follow some of these posts, I started receiving similar posts in my e-mail ID as spam messages. Although I found it quite baffling, I thought it could be just a coincidence.

In 2009 a woman started stacking me online and also over phone. I received a series of calls from a woman claiming to be Swapna from Bangalore. Sometimes the woman told me that she was working as an executive at Google India office, while at other times she said she was working at Facebook. The woman started calling me from different phone numbers, each time giving a different name such as Swapna, Jyoti, Kiran, Savita etc. It was quite obvious that it was the same woman, since the voice, accent, style and intonation was the same. It was also obvious that she was stalking me for an ulterior motive, since a Google or Facebook executive would have little to do with someone like me who had hardly any presence on social media.

During the years 2011 and 2012 there was a marked reduction in the stalking activity of this woman. So I had largely forgotten aouut those spam calls and messages. But then suddenly in September 2013 a woman named Chitrangdha K Ganesh sent me a message on Poemhunter website. The title of her message read "I am bowled over by your poetic skills". It was very perplexing. I

In August 2013 I had exposed certain fraudulent activities in the online Poemhunter Poetry Competition, in which I was a participant. I found that out of the 100 poems reaching the final, 37 appeared to be the works of same person. The poems showed exquisite craftsmanship and were on wide ranging topics. But all these 37 poems had a typical signature style.

Many of these poems had been submitted by poets with similar names such as Prem Kumar, Prem Jyot, Prem123 etc. I had lodged a written complaint with Poemhunter.com website regarding such fraud, but received no response.

When I received the mail from Chitrangdha initially I thought as if the sender had some divine connection with me. But immediately I remembered the Poemhunter fraud, and thought this woman could be connected with that episode. Either the woman herself was the fraudster, or maybe some Poemhunter staff investigating the fraud. So I was wary of disclosing any details about me to this woman.

Although initially I avoided the woman, she kept on sending me her e-mail IDs and mobile numbers, requesting me to share my contact details. Although I was wary of the woman, finally curiosity got the better of me. I did some online chatting with the woman on Poemhunter platform. She introduced herself to me as a freelance worker in the field of advertisement and tourism. However after some time she started contradicting her own statements. Sometimes she said she was a researcher, a student, and IT professional or even a journalist. Sometimes she said she was married, and sometimes unmarried. Sometimes she said she was 39 years old, and at other times 33 or 43.

In April-May 2014 "Chitrangdha" obtained from me my mobile number and called me. In her very first call she told me about her life-long desire to study the Rg Veda and Qu'ran. She also told me that one day she would like to come to my house to study the Veda and Qu'ran with me. I found it quite surprising. Because ever since my childhood I had an unusual interest in the scriptures, and I had particular fascination for the rhythmic mantras of Rg Veda and Sama Veda as well as for the melodious Ayats of Quran as rendered by the Muezzins in mosques.

I developed a very intimate online relationship with this Chitrangdha. She was the first person with whom I had any personal chats online. She exchanged hundreds of messages with me via Facebook, WhatsApp,

Poemhunter, SMS and other media. Sometimes she would call me up to ten times in a day. Often she told me that it was her life-long desire to come to my house and spend the rest of her life with me. I found t very strange. I suspected of a past life connection with her.

On June 5, 2015 Chitrangdha revealed to me that her actual name was Hemangi Sharma, and that she was a student at National Institute of Rural Development, Hyderabad. She also admitted that she had been trolling me since 2009 under a series of fake IDs. She said she came to know about me from a person named Basant Kumar Rath, a senior police officer posted in Jammu. This Basant Rath was my childhood friend and had studied with me in the same class up to university level. Hemangi Sharma aka Chitrangdha had been born and brought up in Jammu before she moved to Bangalore and Hyderabad for job.

In July 2015 I met Hemangi Sharma at her office in Hyderabad. She had invited me to participate in the annual convocation ceremony of her institute. She had booked a room for me in her office guest house. I spent two days with her. During those two days she shared with me her life story. She also discussed the hidden secrets of various world scriptures including the Bible and the Qu'ran. The religious philosophies that Hemangi Sharma discussed with me are the same that Antony Theodore has described in detail in his Christian poems.

When I met Hemangi Sharma in person she did not admit that she was Antony Theodore. But she admitted that she had hundreds of fake IDs. She showed me how she had created multiple Ids by using different mobile phones and SIM cards. But when I asked her to open Chitrangdha's e-mail, she said she had forgotten Chitra's password. When I asked her why she had opened so many fake IDs, she said that she had worked as a marketing executive at Google and Facebook, and that sending spam advertisements to unsuspecting customers was part of her lucrative corporate job. She also said that she had got fed up with that kind of artificial and unethical job, and therefore she had quit the job to pursue a career in rural development.

Initially Hemangi Sharma had shared with me those IDs through whch she had been sending spam mails. But after I came back from Hyderabad, Hemangi Sharma gradually revealed to me her other IDs under which she had posted thousands of poems online. Then only I realised Hemangi Sharma's true stature as a world class poet. I was surprised that she had not published even a single poem under her own name. All her poems had been published under hundreds of pseudonyms. After introducing me to her poetry, Hemangi Sharma deactivated her original e-mail IDs. So I was forced to correspond with her via her fake IDs. She discussed her poetry with me in great detail over thousands of messages exchanged through such fake IDs. And then one fine day she deleted all her messages to me. That left me with no evidence that she had indeed discussed her poetry with me. However I managed to save a few of those messages as proof of her correspondence with me.

Hemangi Sharma has uploaded thousands of her poems in different languages under hundreds of fake IDs. She is a multi-linguist with scholarly understanding of all major world religions. One fails to understand why a spiritual person like her would use so many fake IDs, which is a criminal offence. But then strange are the ways of the devotees of God.

When Hemangi Sharma first started corresponding with me, I immediately knew that she was the person behind the hundreds of fake IDs under which she had uploaded her poems. However she admitted to it much later, only after I relentlessly pursued her to know the truth. She has the talent and creativity to write spontaneously in thousands of different styles. But there were certain underlying patterns in all her works. The most common element in her writings is her use of small "i" to denote the first person singular. She purportedly did so to underplay the individual ego in the creative process. But there is still no plausible explanation for the use of thousands of fake IDs. She could have adopted a single pseudonym to mask her identity, but she chose to have thousands. I believe that she wrote under fake IDs to completely dissociate her ego from the creative process. I myself had resorted to such a technique during my student days. I found that the poems I had written under pseudonyms were qualitatively much better than those published under my real name.

Another underlying pattern in Hemangi Sharma's writings is her utter disregard for the conventional rules of grammar. Among all her online avatars, I found Dr Tony Brahmin (Antony Theodore) as comparatively the most conventional one in terms of style. Lalitha Iyer was a mixture of conventional style and unconventional word play. However certain freedom in use of language can also be seen in Antony's poems.

Yet another frequent feature in Hemangi Sharma's writings is the use of abbreviations, colloquial expressions and liberal use of nouns as verbs and adjectives. For instance she would write "RV Lovers" instead of "Are We in Love". You is abbreviated to "u" in most of her writings. Instead of "more childish", she will simply write "childer". For instance, in one of her letters to me, she wrote "love makes heart become childer". Even mobile SMS texts such as Gn and Tc (goodnight, take care etc) frequently appear in her poems. She also uses past, present and future tenses in the same poem as part of the same dialogue between protagonists. This reflects her belief that time is an illusion, and that earthly concept of time does not exist at all in the realm of God consciousness.

What makes her art so special is that she makes such unusual expressions quite spontaneously. The reader hardly suspects that she is deliberately doing so. Classical English expressions gladly coexist with ultra-modern sms texts.

In addition to "Antony", Hemangi Sharma has also adopted other interesting pseudonyms such as Lalitha Iyer, Dev Anand, Poet Poet, Sun Princess, April Pearl and a host of other IDs. She has used both male and female names, as well as names from different languages. She has used Hindu names, Christian names and Muslim names. Maybe she did so to identify herself with all humanity irrespective of artificial barriers created by gender, race, caste, language and religion.

But still she could have managed to do all this with 30 or 40 IDs. I really don't know what could have been Hemangi Sharma's real intention in adopting hundreds and thousands of fake IDs. Any discerning reader would have noticed the underlying pattern in the poems written under different IDs. But perhaps nobody pointed it out before I did so. I was the only person who lodged a written complaint regarding her fake IDs. Perhaps Hemangi Sharma deliberately did so with the expectation that someday someone would find out her real identity. Perhaps it was God's design that I would become that person. Or maybe it was Hemangi Sharma's own design – who knows?

Hemangi Sharma had frequently expressed to me her desire to open a school for underprivileged children, and also to adopt a baby girl with my financial support. She wanted to have an unconventional school, which would be completely free from the curriculum of rote learning. She told me that she wanted me as the Mentor of her "school". I do not know what exactly was in my mind. I asked her to explain to me her idea of "mentor". But she was evasive in her answers. However, from the very beginning of her interactions with me she clearly told me about her disapproval of abortion of foetses. Protection of children and their precious childhood was her topmost priority, and it took up bulk of her conversations with me. She said she had left her lucrative corporate job to take up the study of rural development solely for the purpose of empowering vulnerable women and underprivileged children.

But from my extensive discussions with her I clearly understood that whenever she was talking about abortion she was not limiting the concept to only physical killing of the physical fetus inside a woman's womb. She was more concerned about the overall spiritual evolution of mankind. Abandonment of spiritual quest is also akin to killing of the spiritual embryo growing inside a devotee's heart. Protecting the physical embryo inside the womb is symbolic of the continuation of devotion to God.

Tapan Kumar Pradhan

APPENDIX

ANTONY THEODORE

POEMS IN TRANSLATION

IF YOU DIE BEFORE ME

Do you mean when you see a better beauty, you shall leave me?
Oh dear, you mean to say you will die before me?
Now what to say, I shall thank God for your being with me so long.
And then, I will suffer.
I shall end my life if there is no children to be taken care of.
When you die, I shall also die, no more happily united with you.
I was a lost soul.
Till I met you
Till I found my god.

MOM'S SMILES

Very sentimental poetry....
I recall my mom's last eyes....
no tears....
Smiles as she passed by
tears did not then come into my eyes I too smiled
Then it rained all day and night
mom's smiles went away
now I thirst for those looks till today
as she passed away

it rains till today
nearly five decades away
she still smiles daily at me
I my mom can see
smiling with me

It does no longer rain
now it only snows
heaven knows
when she calls out to me
when are you coming?
I smile back and ask
Are you still waiting for me?

MOM'S LAST SMILE
(Translated into German by the poet)

Das Lächeln meiner Mutter

Das Lächeln der Mütter
Ein Gedicht von mir, dem Dichter Yeps

Das Lächeln meiner Mutter
Ist mein Gedicht der Klassik
Viele haben es gelobt
Über alle Grenzen hinweg

Mach einen Punkt, um es zu lesen
Sie haben ebenfalls eine liebevolle Mutter

Sie kommt immer noch täglich zu mir
Lächelt aufrichtig und ernsthaft
Und sagt
Sohn, ich warte immer noch auf dich
Aber nimm dir Zeit
Ich habe es nicht eilig

Hier gibt es keine Sorgen
Der Herr kümmert sich unentwegt um uns
Voller Ernst
Wie du, mein Sohn, es ebenfalls tust

Aber dich kennenzulernen
Wird mein allumfassendes Verlangen sein
Tief erfüllt
Und verfasse weitere Gedichte
Sie von deinem Sohn zu lesen,
ist ergreifend

Ja, sie ist verstorben
Vor fast 50 Jahren
Ist sie den einsamen Weg allein gegangen

Niemand bleibt auf Erden
Wir alle werden sterben
Aber meine Liebe gilt dir
So lange ich lebe
O Dichter, sie können dir
Alles geben

Ja, sie ist vor fast 50 Jahren den einsamen Lebensweg gegangen.
Niemand bleibt ewig auf Erden. Wir alle werden sterben.
Aber die Liebe ist das größte Geschenk.

Und die Dichter können über sie schreiben.

Note :- This is a free translation of the poem "Mom's Smiles" by Me Poet
Yeps Poet (Antony's/ Hemangi's pseudonym) in a different version..

IF YOU DIE BEFORE ME

If you die before me
I would jump down into your grave
and hug you so innocently
that angels will become jealous

I shall kiss you
So intimately shall I kiss you
that your breath becomes mine
In one breath of love shall
we merge into hugs of true joy

Your heart shall beat
in rhythms unheard
like the drums of the desert
and the wild forest in the night

You shall murmur in my ears:
'Oh press me to your chest;
Tear open your chest,
Make way for me
to enter into your loving heart
that beats only for me in resounding colors

Tell me please Oh my lover
Is it a rainbow that I see?
or the glow of a burning pyre?
Why is it that I cannot utter it in words?
Tell me glorious angels of love:
What am I experiencing in uncountable
moments of indescribable inner comfort?

Shivering in your presence
I shall long to dance with you.

If the dark souls lead you to Hades
I will dance and dance with you
even in the nether world

We shall dance soft and then wild
We shall dance together

as one body and soul
and break the fetters of hell
through love that emanates from our dance

Dance so long and fine like a poem
until the Lords of the dark would faint

Breaking the fetters of Hades
the white angels attired in beauty
shall fly down to pick you up on golden cradles
and carry you to the world of God

So you will be free and fly away
from me into the world of the heavens
where angels shall kiss your sacred body
You will be attired in gold and white
and in varied colors in tune
with the flowers of heaven

Then you need no space to live and breathe

Into that world of purity you will go
and I will be here on earth
dreaming of your joys with
the Heavenly spirits

Shall I wait?

Shall I wait at dusk and dawn
in sobs and a heaving heart
with such desire and passion
to reach you one day
in your world of happiness.

Editor's Note :- The poem is apparently based on the belief that once your
lady love dies before you, she has to go to Hades where she has to dance
fiercely and lovingly to make the Lords of Darkness faint, so that she can
free herself from the chains of hell. However the poem can also be
symbolic of the mother-child relationship. For when the unborn baby is
killed inside the womb, it becomes the first one to depart – and the mother
would have to do all the dancing in hell.

IF YOU DIE BEFORE ME

(Translated into Greek by Mary Skarpathiotaki)

Αν πεθάνεις πριν από εμένα

Αν πεθάνεις πριν από εμένα
Ποίημα από τον Δρ. Αντώνη Θεόδωρο

Αν πεθάνεις πριν από εμένα
Θα εισχωρούσα στον τάφο σου
και να σας αγκαλιάσω τόσο αθώα
ότι οι άγγελοι θα ζηλεύουν.

Θα σε φιλήσω.
Θα σε φιλήσω τόσο θερμά
ώσπου η αναπνοή σου να γίνει δική μου.
Με μία αναπνοή αγάπης θα
μετουσιωνόμασταν σε αγκαλιές αληθινής χαράς.

Η καρδιά σου θα χτυπούσε
σε ρυθμούς ανήκουστης μελωδίας
όπως τα τύμπανα της ερήμου
και το άγριο δάσος τη νύχτα.

Θα ψυθιρίζατε στα αυτιά μου:
«Ω, σφίξτε με στο στήθος σας.
Δάκρυα θα ανοίξουν το στήθος σας
θα ανοίξουν οδό για μένα
να εισχωρήσω στην αγαπημένη σας καρδιά
που χτυπά μόνο για μένα σε ηχηρά χρώματα.

Πες μου παρακαλώ Αγάπη μου
Είναι ένα ουράνιο τόξο που βλέπω
ή τη λάμψη μιας πυρκαγιάς που φλέγεται
Γιατί δεν μπορώ να το λέω με λέξεις
Πες μου λαμπρέ άγγελε αγάπης:
Τι βιώνω σε αμέτρητες
στιγμές απερίγραπτης εσωτερικής ευφορίας

Δρασκελώντας με την παρουσία σας

Θα ήθελα πολύ να χορέψω μαζί σας.

Αν σκοτεινές ψυχές σας οδηγήσουν στον Άδη
Θα χορέψω και θα χορέψω μαζί σας
ακόμα και στον κόσμο.

Θα χορέψουμε απαλά και στη συνέχεια έντονα.
Θα χορέψουμε μαζί
ως ένα σώμα και ψυχή
και να σπάσει τα δεσμά της κόλασης
μέσω της αγάπης που προέρχεται από τον χορό μας.

Χορός σε διάρκεια και ωραίος σαν ποίημα
μέχρις ότου οι Κύριοι του σκοταδιού εξασθενίσουν.

Σπάζοντας τα δεσμά του Άδη
οι λευκοί άγγελοι που ενδύονται με ομορφιά
θα πετάξουν για να σε πάρει σε χρυσά λίκνα
και να σας μεταφέρει στον κόσμο του Θεού.

Έτσι θα είστε ελεύθεροι και πετάτε μακριά
από μένα, στον κόσμο των ουρανών
όπου οι άγγελοι θα φιλήσουν το ιερό σώμα σου.
Θα βρεθείτε σε χρυσό και λευκό
και σε ποικίλα χρώματα σε μελωδία
με τα λουλούδια του ουρανού.

Τότε δεν χρειάζεται χώρος για να ζήσεις και να αναπνεύσεις.

Σε αυτόν τον κόσμο της αγνότητας θα πάτε
και θα είμαι εδώ στη γη
ονειρεύεστε τις χαρές σας με
τα ουράνια πνεύματα.

Πρέπει να περιμένω
Πρέπει να περιμένω το σούρουπο και την αυγή
σε αναγνώσεις και σε μια βαριά καρδιά
με τέτοια επιθυμία και πάθος
για να σας φτάσω μια μέρα
στον κόσμο της ευτυχίας.

www.ingramcontent.com/pod-product-compliance
Lightning Source LLC
LaVergne TN
LVHW010520200726
843506LV00013B/2654